MEDITATION, MYSTICISM AND THE MYSTERY

To Inner Perception and Understanding

LUCIENE AZIQUE

AurA Press

Published by
AurA PRESS
2 Francis Street
Leicestern LE2 2BD

Published by AurA Press
1995

British Library Cataloging in Publication Data

ISBN 0 9523144 0 1

Printed in Great Britain by
Castle
Glasgow

My Lord Jesus

You came to me on the rays of the Sun,
Your knowledge, Beauty and Enlightenment.
Your Spirit pervaded my heart,
Teaching it the expansion of Your Wisdom,
Truth and Realisation;
My heart filled with an overflowing Love,
When I perceived Your Invisible Form,
Standing in the clouds.
Your Light brilliantly cast down
Upon the earth;
Erasing the darkness.
And Your Light when it filled my room,
Your Spirit was with me.
You teach me by Your Wisdom,
Your clear-sighted Truth,
Knowledge and Unity.
I am with You, My Lord,
In the zenith of your Bliss.
When my cup over-filled with
Your Knowledge,
I have found ecstasy in You,
In Your words and invisibility.
I can also feel You coming closer to me,
Gliding on the sun's gossamer ray;
Filling my Soul with Your Love,
And Your wisdom in my mind,
Taking away all Illusion from within me.

Christ The Messiah

Come share my Joy, oh you people of the world.
I have found Christ, On a single beam of Light,
Coming from Heaven.

I now know that I have Conquered the Devil,
And the Temptations of the world.
I have found the Path; Straight and narrow,
True and Sublime;
Which led me to the Light; Transferring from Heaven
Into my heart.

I cry for You, As I have cried for Aeons;
So that Your knowledge; Is spread to every heart.

I seek for You to come To this world;
That all may know You, As I know You.

Your Love Brings tears to my eyes,
Elation coursing through my Soul'
I am aware you exist; Just a step away,
A door from the visible Into the invisible.

Your reality comes to me; Passing through me,
Into the written Word; The Word of God,
Of Present, Past and The Everlasting Life.
There are tears in my eyes, and bliss in my heart;
As this Knowledge, of the Word of God Appears before me.

My Quest has been forever, but now I am seeing You,
Appearing, tangibly.
Understanding Your Perception,
Which forever has been steeped in Esoteric Mystery.

ACKNOWLEDGEMENTS

Edwin C Steinbrecher, author of *THE INNER GUIDE TO MEDITATION*, whose work inspired me to write this book.

Ken Carey, author of *STARSEED, THE THIRD MILLENIUM*, whose work helped me to awaken.

To all the Light-workers and specially to my known and unknown Guides for their specialised knowledge on the inner planes.

To my children who have been supportive and to Julia Isaacs for illustrating the Archetypes.

To my eldest son Marcus, who has been supportive. To my youngest son Jason, for his picture of the Madonna. To my friend Julie Isaacs, for helping me in creating the illustrations. To my parents.

Lastly to my other helpers who have made this production possible.

Salutation for the Light
and to the Divine Presence Within

SEPHIROTH

The Spheres mentioned herein are related to the
Qabalistic Tree of Life;
these energies or experiences not normally available on the
material plane but are encountered in deep meditation.

Malkuth
Hod
Netzach
Tipareth
Yesod
Geburah and Chesed
Chokma
Kether

A GLYPH OF THE QABALAH MEDITATION

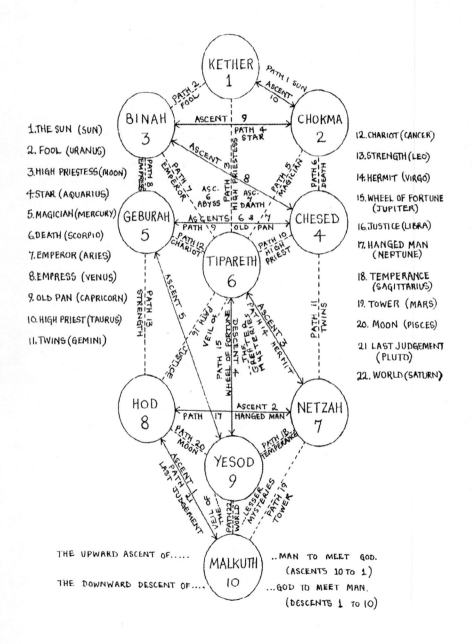

1. THE SUN (SUN)
2. FOOL (URANUS)
3. HIGH PRIESTESS (MOON)
4. STAR (AQUARIUS)
5. MAGICIAN (MERCURY)
6. DEATH (SCORPIO)
7. EMPEROR (ARIES)
8. EMPRESS (VENUS)
9. OLD PAN (CAPRICORN)
10. HIGH PRIEST (TAURUS)
11. TWINS (GEMINI)

12. CHARIOT (CANCER)
13. STRENGTH (LEO)
14. HERMIT (VIRGO)
15. WHEEL OF FORTUNE (JUPITER)
16. JUSTICE (LIBRA)
17. HANGED MAN (NEPTUNE)
18. TEMPERANCE (SAGITTARIUS)
19. TOWER (MARS)
20. MOON (PISCES)
21. LAST JUDGEMENT (PLUTO)
22. WORLD (SATURN)

THE UPWARD ASCENT OF..... ..MAN TO MEET GOD.
(ASCENTS 10 TO 1)

THE DOWNWARD DESCENT OF.... ...GOD TO MEET MAN.
(DESCENTS 1 TO 10)

FOR THE NEW AGE

With the guidance of the Inner Guides and Archetypal
Enlightenment of the Twenty-Two Aspects of God on the
Spiritual Path

If it were not for them and for all their profound wisdom I would
not fly with the White Eagle in the Realms of the Sublime

CONTENTS

MEDITATION, MYSTICISM AND THE MYSTERY

THE INTRODUCTION

If you seriously seek your Spiritual Path, I recommend that you read and study the book, *The Inner Guide Meditation*, by **E.C. Steinbrecher**. Through it, I have achieved an insight of my own spirituality. It has fanned the dying embers of my soul into a gigantic flame.

I will outline the procedure I use to prepare my body for meditation, as you may wish to follow it. You may of course use another method. Whatever preparation you use, it is imperative that you use a mental triangle in the mind's eye, visually employing changing colours on its angles. If the colours given below do not suit you, choose those that make you feel most comfortable.

Sit upright, with your spine relaxed and the head supported. Your legs should be uncrossed, feet flat on the floor. Rest your hand lightly on the thighs, palms upwards. Close your eyes and concentrate seeing the darkness in your head. Breathe deeply, slowly and rhythmically, consciously eradicating the ever-swirling thoughts. In the deep dark depths of your mind imagine you are moving forward, then left and right. Visualise a mental triangle. Now move your mind forwards to the angle on the right and then upwards to the apex. Next move to the angle at the bottom left and finally project your mind to the angle at the bottom right. Repeat the same sequence around the triangle, forward, top, left then right. Continue in a flowing rhythm around the triangle, associating a colour with each movement; electric-blue for forward, scarlet for the left and daffodil-yellow for the right.

Continue moving about the mental triangle until you are no longer aware of yourself. When you are completely relaxed and in touch with the inner dimension create a new visual field. Create a cave in your new visual field and move into it, in whatever shape or form you like. Don't imagine it, but see it with your own eyes as if you are actually there in your own body. Look at your hands and feet, feel the floor beneath you, smell the air, see the light, touch the texture and listen intently for any sounds.

Pick up and sift all the information. Use every sense, every faculty. At the same time discard the ego and let your real self take control.

Walk into the cave and stand very still. When you have observed every detail of your new surroundings, look for a doorway or an opening to the left of you. If there is no exit visible, just walk straight through the cave's wall.

You have stepped into the strange landscape, where you will meet your 'Spiritual Animal'. Call it softly and gently using your inner voice. It will come. Do not accept any mythical animal such as a griffin or unicorn etc., or your cat or dog or any known pet from your physical world.

Command the spiritual animal to take you to your inner guide. Always follow it to the right, for if you wander to the left a false guide will come. Once you have been introduced to the genuine guide your spiritual animal will automatically disappear.

THE MENTAL TRIANGLE

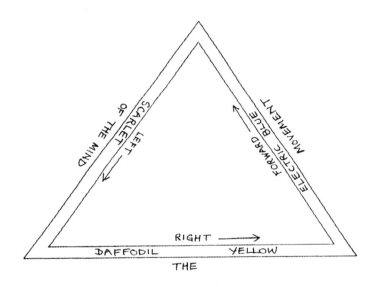

THE
GEOPHYSICAL ORBICULAR DIMENSION

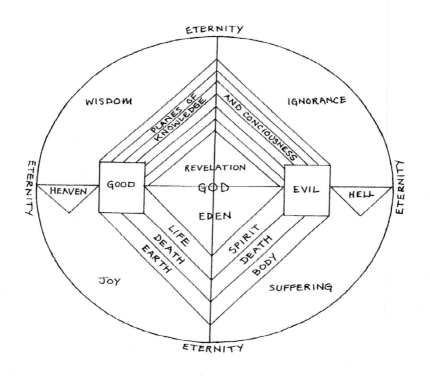

THE MEDITATION

The guide is your direct link with your inner-self. Through his influence you will realise a different reality. He has the wisdom to put you in touch with your twenty-two aspects of God. At the same time he will interact with you in your inner and daily life. I have chosen the Tarot archetypal forces to represent these aspects, but you can choose whatever you fancy: For example Walt Disney characters, Alice in Wonderland people, or biblical characters as your archetypes.

Each archetype-entity will give you a gift, place it somewhere in your body and tell you its meaning or significance.

I will describe the my own meditation experiences: Once I had moved into the cave I stood very still. The light inside was dim and it was rather cool. I noticed there was another entrance, just opposite. I walked over to it and peered outside. It was a rocky-mountainside leading down to a deserted beach. Dotted along the rock-face were several caves. Coarse patchy green grass grew beside the gravel paths leading down to the white-sands below. A bright yellow sun blazed in a deep blue sky.

I retreated to back into the cave and looked for a doorway on my left. There being none I pushed against the hard wall. Miraculously, I passed through the wall and stepped onto a straight gravel path which seemed to go on endlessly disappearing into the horizon. To my right the view was obscured by tall trees and thorny-shrubs. To the left was a clearing and beyond that a huge forest.

I turned towards the clearing and called for my spiritual animal. A white dove came into my view. I commanded it saying, "Take me to my guide."

It flew into the forest and I followed. It led me to a small circular pool and to a young man, a Red-Indian. He looked about twenty; quite tall, with a muscular, tanned body and long, silky, black hair flowing down to his waist. He was wearing a three-quarter length tunic in white, tied loosely. He wore two dove feathers on his white headband. His feet were bare.

We did not speak. My first impression of him was that he appeared sedate and aloof. I went closer and waited. He addressed me and I was amazed. It was not talk as I knew it. He spoke to me inside my mind saying, "I will communicate by thought-transference." I was fascinated, I could understand. He continued, "I am your guide and my name is Zalmné."

Time of meditation: 5.30 AM 23/9/90

THE SUN - The Illumination

I relaxed, closed my eyes and drifted into the astral-sphere. I saw Zalmné standing by the pool as before. I was cautious; terribly unsure as to what would happen. I was lost and out of my depth. I went to him and took his hand in my right hand. I was very much aware of his masculine presence. In shyness I asked, "Shall we go and search for the Sun-Humanoid?"

Clasped hand in hand we walked. I watched the sun rise in the shimmering sky. I asked the sun to come to me in a human form. In response it replied, "I will not come down to the earth. Come and meet me in the sky."

Suddenly, I was weightless. Soaring above the soft clouds. Sitting next to Zalmné on his white-winged stallion. I wondered where I was for a minute. Am I dreaming? I thought. then I remembered, I was in the inner-astral plane.

We flew to our destination. I was astounded. The Sun was not fiery, hot and blazing. Instead; its composition was soft and yielding. The solar fires were cool, and the flames were a smoky-blue and transparent. It seemed we were drifting through a spiritual-substance making up its yellow and blue heart.

I asked, "Which gift are you placing in my body? What do you want of me?"

The Sun replied, "I will give you a dazzling quartz crystal, four inches in length, and place it in the cavity of your heart. Once embedded, it will give you much clarity of thought. A great love will come. Things which are hidden from you know will be made known. The crystal will glow within you and radiate a rainbow. This will be your arch to the new world. Its knowledge will take you to distant lands past troubled waters and mysterious shores."

He placed the crystal in my heart. Instantly, things became clearer. I was aware of a power flowing outwards from inwards, creating within me harmony and tranquillity. I stood transfixed in breathless wonder. I felt as if I was embarking on a great adventure. A new, whole, profound reality was mine to be grasped and explored.

I was overwhelmed as a feeling of elation welled deep within me. I was joyful and thankful. I had succeeded in conquering the ego which separates spiritual and worldly realities.

I said farewell to my Zalmné and passed through the cave to be reunited with my physical body.

Time of meditation: 1 PM 23/9/90

On my third visit to my guide
We were standing side by side
And these words were inspired:

FOOL

Peruse and see this love,
In flight free like the dove,
Flowing calm and pure,
Transparent bright and sure.

The entities they gather here,
To be freed of their fear,
Many will drink from this Well,
They will their wisdom tell.

In harmony in the mystical night,
Is as magical as the moon-light,
All this wondrous love to share,
In a secret dream - will anyone dare?

Date of meditation: 23/9/90

THE FOOL - The Light

I relaxed once more into the meditation and found myself beside the pool, with the help of the spiritual dove. When I saw Zalmné I said, "I would like to meet the High Priestess."

We walked through the greenwood; stopping beside a large, glassy, still lake. Zalmné commented, "This is where she lives but she tells me by telepathy, she cannot see you until you have seen the Fool. Without his special light, you will be unable to cross the frontiers of the spiritual-realm. Without his initiation, you will be lost in the wilderness of your path. The way will be dark and you will be sad and lonely in your quest."

Zalmné and I retreated to the dense undergrowth. We searched deeper and deeper in the shadowy forest. Then I saw a translucent viridian phantom snaking and coiling around the trees and branches. It had a face of a man with a flimsy ghostly body which entwined and encircled the huge trunks of giant trees. His companions, were elves. These mischievous luminous fairies played between the trees.

I asked, "Which gift are you placing in my body. And what do you need in return?"

The Fool, producing a glittering two inch emerald and pointing to my forehead and said, "I am putting this emerald into your third eye. It will give you the light. Its light will shine brightly on the inner planes, showing you your path. Now that I have initiated you, go back to the High Priestess, she will give you her wise counsel."

Date of meditation: 23/9/90 - 7-00 PM

THE HIGH PRIESTESS - The Psychic

Zalmné and I returned through the thick foliage to the abode of the High Priestess. She was still reluctant to reveal herself. She spoke, shrouded in her mystic veil. "Wait for me by the water - I will join you."

Whilst we waited for her to emerge from her misty shadows; the swans upon the lake came forward. They said, "Do not be impatient, the Lady will be with you soon."

When she did; I was dazzled by her beauty. I held my breath in wonder. She was majestic. Her silver gown outshone the silver light of the moon; sparkling brilliantly like the jewelled sky. The I saw she was cradling a baby, lovingly and tenderly.

"I am Mary," she addressed me, "I have come down from the higher plane to give you my guidance. Firstly, you had to be initiated by the Fool to receive my wisdom. The truth can blind those who are ignorant. Your darkness was dispelled by the Fool's light. Now you will be able to perceive the hidden knowledge." She paused, "Wisdom is hard to attain but one who seeks and thirsts for truth will be revealed."

I was mesmerised by her radiant beauty and completely in love with her. I asked for the gift and what she needed from me in return.

"I am putting a silver wand through your eyes. Any darkness you possess now will be totally obliterated. When your eyes open again your sight will be even clearer than before. The spiritual path you tread will be lit by the Fool's light and my psychic silver wand will aid you in your arduous journey."

I was overcome by her speech and profoundly elated.

Zalmné and I returned to the pool. After a short while, I said farewell and reunited with my physical body.

Date of meditation: 23/9/90 - 10.00 PM

THE STAR - The Alien

Zalmné was waiting for my arrival, standing beside the pool. We conversed by thought-transference. All my inner channels opened in readiness to receive his thoughts. Our minds united binding us together in a unique, invisible structure.

I asked him to take me to the Star. He obliged and we searched for the Star-Humanoid.

We found him on the tranquil seascape. He was rather tall about seven foot. His face resembled a human, but it was elongated like an anteater's. His huge scaly-wings were grey and shiny. He suggested a trip to his Star-Land. I agreed and clambered inside the oblong crystal cubicle set between his shoulder blades.

He flapped his gigantic wings and we were airborne flying in the glory of the evening sky. When finally we landed on a star, I was inwardly surprised. I had imagined a most attractive starscape, but as I looked around, I saw only dismal grey-rock formations. Desolate, isolate and bitterly cold! The Star-Alien sensed my reaction: and he said, "The beauty you see in the stars from your earth's sphere is the light of the ephemeral sun."

I asked, "Which gift are you putting in my body and what is its significance?"

He produced a small smooth stone saying: "This pebble is from my home. Hold it tightly in your right hand. It has the power to transmit love. You will share joy with all you meet. Your bond will become greater and love will blossom between you and your guide. Building upon your aspirations of hopes and optimism. It will strengthen you as you follow your chosen path." The Star-Alien brought us back to the astral world and then he left us. I said farewell to Zalmné and reunited with my physical body.

Time of meditation: 11.00 PM 23/9/90

THE MAGICIAN - The Unknown

This time we searched for the Magician. We walked together until we arrived at a boiling, bubbling lake; set against a background of high, dark looming cliffs. The water was turbulent, hissing and steaming. In the middle there were four dragons: Three small ones and a huge serpent-snake betwixt them. They were bellowing and spitting flames and sulphur-ash in the already hazy smoky atmosphere.

An old man came forward from the misty shadows. He wore a heavy hooded grey robe. His twinkling, grey-blue eyes were full of mirth. He had very fine long white hair and a similar beard to complement. At a glance I could see he was full of irresistible charm and magnetism. His skin hung loose on his pale features, and a transparent glimmering white light surrounded his frame.

I asked the Old Magician, "Which gift are you putting in my body and what is its purpose?"

"I hold in my hand a pentacle," he replied," I will put it in your belly. Once it has dissolved and has been absorbed; you will know the unknown and have knowledge of the physical, spiritual and inner planes."

As the pentacle began to dissolve, I grasped the meaning of the seven lamps lit in each of the seven caves, dotted around the Magician's lake. 'The lamps represented seven manifestations .

Zalmné and I returned to the pool. I realised our love was increasing. It was so undemanding and pure. So often now, I do not want to return to my physical body. I want to remain the inner world. But Zalmné says, "You must return. I exist solely for your protection, so that you are unharmed

by the inner travels."
I said farewell and through the cave returned to my meditating body.
Time of meditation: 12.00 AM 23/9/90

THE DEATH - The Kundalini

I met Zalmné at the pool-side. He was very quiet and unresponsive. The contact between us was fuzzy; but like the fog lifting over the sea; the inner images cleared and focused. The ego receded to the unconscious to let me fully submerge in the domain of the conscious meditation.

Zalmné watched me walking towards him. He stepped out of the water. I noticed he was holding two black mambas, one encircled around each arm. He seemed withdrawn and unapproachable - as though, it was a tremendous effort to speak. By sign only, he gesticulated,"Follow me." I obeyed without hesitation. I trusted him completely..

We walked to the Land of the Magi. The Old Magician was waiting for us. He was uncommunicative as well. By a wave of his hand he indicated that I was to follow. I followed them both into a dark tunnel. In the darkness it seemed we were levitating at a great speed.

Fear gripped me. My heart palpitated echoing in my head. A tight constriction knotted in my gut. Paralysis numbed my brain. I could hardly breathe and death-death pounded all around me!

We levitated faster and deeper. Suddenly, without any warning a massive cobra rose up. The diameter of its head was six-foot across and its body trailed a long way, disappearing in the darkness. It was grotesque, hissing and spitting at us; not letting us pass!

By this time I was petrified! I remained conscious and did not collapse in the disintegration of my very own personal dread. Nevertheless, I was weak, exhausted and drained. The force of the experience was powerful. Zalmné and the Old Magician pulled me away, guiding me back to the golden light.

Once my tranquillity was somewhat restored, I asked Zalmné, "What was that?" He replied, "Death, disguised as a serpent. He is the guardian of the inner esoteric plane. Whoever takes this path must meet the snake. The fear has to be conquered before any real progress is made on the spiritual journey. Many obstacles have to be overcome to go further."

I moaned, "It was really frightening!" Zalmné replied, "Go and lie in the cool water. Your equilibrium will soon return." I relaxed in the enchanting pool and immediately equanimity returned.

For the second time, I questioned him, "Why did I meet the snake?"
He answered, "The kundalini lies coiled within you. The experience of death tests the strength of the spirit. Once it is made conscious within you, the living spirit uncoils to work with the inner-self to define the deeper

14

mysteries." He placed the two black mambas in the water and they swam away hurriedly.

I said farewell and reunited with my other body.

Date of meditation: 24/9/90 PM

THE EMPEROR - The Father

I went to the pool but did not see Zalmné standing or sitting in the usual place. I waited for him. A short time passed and then I saw him sauntering out of the woods. He had a young deer slung over the back of his shoulders. Pointing to it he said, "We will eat."

Whilst the deer-meat spit-roasted and crackled over the fire, we conversed. I spoke in frustration, "Why is it so difficult to identify myself in the inner world?"

Zalmné offered a solution, "I would like you to wear a green silk dress. Put it on as soon as you enter this dimension. This will help combine the realities of the two worlds."

We shared the meat and then rested; enjoying the companionship and the silence. At last I broke it by saying, "I would like to visit the Emperor."

We walked through the forest. In the distance I saw a powerful stallion. It came nearer and nearer and suddenly stopped in front of us. A dignified Indian chief was seated on it. He looked about fifty, very proud and austere. He was wearing a glorious head-dress. He had painted his face and torso in magnificent bright colours with designs of eagles. He addressed me saying,

"I am the father of Zalmné."

I was a bit surprised that Zalmné had a father, nevertheless, I made no comment. He continued,"My son has acquired much wisdom which in due course will impart to you."

I asked what gift he would give me.

He answered, "I will pluck a feather from my head-dress and put it on your right arm. It will bring you much happiness. It has the power to protect you from any negative archetypes and harnesses an understanding of all that is and exists."

Zalmné and I accompanied him to his settlement. When we arrived at the peaceful camp, the father remarked, "The land is restful, the tribes are in unity." With that he mounted his horse and galloped towards them.

We returned to the pool and talked. I confided, "When I am here, I find it difficult to return to my physical world, and yet; when I am there, it is difficult to resume the meditation. I avoid meditating become lazy and make excuses; I am too busy!"

"In your world you are pulled by two forces. The negative pull of the earthly world which keeps the ego tied to its 'material strings'. The positive pull of the inner dimension makes the ego lose its influence over the self. Without that conflict, the astral world is much more tangible, that is why you want to remain here." Zalmné explained.

He continued, "I exist solely to protect you in the inner world. I will guide you safely through the traumatic passage. It is my responsibility to see that you are not harmed on these treacherous plains. You are here to learn from the experience, and to apply it in your daily living. The inner is for in-depth exploration within; the burden of physicality has to be endured until death Then you will fly with the White Eagle, forever, in all dimensions."

I stayed with him for a long time. Being with him was extremely pleasant. Then I returned to my physical world via the cave.

Date of meditation: 25/9/90 PM

THE EMPRESS - The Love

I met Zalmné by the waters of the pool. He was swimming. I sensed his mood to be light and cheerful. Our love was bonding perfectly as the Star-Alien had predicted.

He smiled and made me welcome. "Come," he said, "we will swim together."

I said,"I would like to visit the Empress?"

We were still swimming in the pool and I happened to glance to the opposite bank. A beautiful woman was standing there looking at us. She waved and beckoned - "Follow me." She was dressed in a cream satin gown. Glistening pearls sparkled on it like early morning dew.

We followed her to a palace and into a long corridor to the Empress' throne. She was waiting for us and said, "Welcome - I knew you were coming."

She reminded me of Queen Cleopatra, endowed with an abundant grace and elegance. Her features were smooth and aquiline. She wore her jet black hair swept back and tied in a bun . Huge deep blue eyes gazed at me calm and unwavering. Her crown was cast in white gold; hand-carved with designs of snakes, dragons and eagles. Large sapphires and rubies deep-set in the platinum; glittered in the sunlight.

She continued, "The Emperor has given me all this wealth. I in return give him all my love. My love is worth more than all of his gold. The love of gold has no value." I asked for her gift and what was its significance.

"I am giving you a two-inch white diamond and will put it in your solar plexus. Its radiance will shine eternally and its fire will rekindle your passion to unite with the kundalini. Its heart stores the knowledge of the thousand suns, immeasurable in time and space. This rare wisdom you will amass within you."

Zalmné and I returned to the pool. The time came for us to part. I did not

DEATH

EMPEROR

want to leave him.   I wanted to stay here, He sensed my mood and spoke.
"You must go now, your physical world is waiting for you."

Date of meditation: 25/9/90 3.30 PM

A PLEASANT INTERLUDE - of Inspiration

I was out walking,
I stood on the bridge,
Over the Grand Union Canal.
It was late afternoon,
The refraction of the sun caught my eye;
I was transfixed by the Beauty.
The scene bathed in a luminary light;
Ethereal spectres cascaded in the luminosity.
I searched deeper in the watery reflection,
I was as one with the whole.
The existence of physical reality,
Drowned in its depths.
I submerged to drink deep of the Waters Divine,
The trees were adorned with their Special Beauty,
All forms blended with the Perfect Harmony,
All shapes mingled with the One Whole;
The Waters were calm and tranquil,
The trees were laden with Autumn berries,
Harmonising to the complete Unity,
Uniting combining to the deepest mystery,
Of unseen waters that flow.
I continued walking through St Andrew's Churchyard;
I was especially aware of the physical - the Self and the Ego,
All separated from their rigidity,
Each an unknown entity.
I was impressed by this Perception,
The reality was different on this plane,
Not in a fixed state;
But where form flows into form,
Becoming transient in its state of transition.
The I discarded its illusion,
And unification was to catch and behold.
The trees moved with the movement of the Wind,
The leaves drifted down,
Energetic Motion swirled them around,
The rain made them sodden,
They became as one with the Earth.

The process of Death and Birth begins again.

Date of meditation: 28/9/90

THE OLD PAN - The Lust

I met Zalmné by the waters of the pool. He seemed unusually quiet. He addressed me immediately and remarked, "You have not come for a few days?"

"I have been very busy with childminding. I have a real problem with the little boy. He doesn't stop crying. I have to be in the same room with him all the time, otherwise he starts screaming!" I continued, "The other problem is a business proposal someone has put forward, I don't know what to do about it?"

"Don't worry about these trivial things," he replied kindly. "They will sort themselves out." We started walking in the forest, heading for the Land of the Magi. I saw the Old Magician wielding his awesome power, harnessing the portent force of the four dragons.

We saw the Star-Alien alone on his calm seashore. Then we passed the Fool's Land and watched the little elves repairing the forest damage. We stopped at the large tranquil lake and admired its sparkling brightness. The High Priestess waved and smiled as we strolled by.

Zalmné commanded his stallion. Instantly, it obeyed his call and was beside us. We rode deeper and deeper in the dark shadowy undergrowth. The light became dim and dismal. An unnatural odour permeated the atmosphere. Thick swirling mist clung around the ghostly trees. Half-alive bodies hung from the branches, writhing and moaning in agony. Three ugly cackling witches guarded the entrance to the devil's caverns, making evil potions brewing in their cauldron and muttering dark incantations.

Zalmné broke the silence and spoke, "Come, we will go inside. I will protect you." The demon witches did not raise an objection and let us pass freely. We stepped inside. The putrid smell filled our nostrils. A pungent and strong mixture of excrement and stale blood. Then I saw the Devil at the far end of the cave and he was gorging on a still-steaming human heart!

I watched in horror and recoiled at the sight of the slurping oozing red-liquid as it spurted out in short bursts. The Devil's mouth dripped in crimson. He looked up angrily and enquired, "What do you want?"

"Nothing." I replied, overcome with fear.

Then I saw all the naked women sprawled on the ground. The Devil had gratified his lust with each of them. Creamy, frothy semen trickled out from their orifices. I was repulsed and felt sickened by this contemptuous sight. Even so, I had to make a tremendous effort to control the overpowering urge of lust welling up within me.

Zalmné gesticulated for us to leave. We mounted his white-winged stallion and soared in the black star-spangled sky. Many symbols of magic and mysticism floated around us as we drifted carefree in the inner apace.

We returned to the pool. I relaxed for a short while in the clear transparent water. Then I said farewell and reunited with my meditating body.

Time of meditation: 1/10/90

THE HIGH PRIEST - The Mystic

I walked towards the familiar pool, but today I was a little bit uneasy. Like animals before the onset of a storm, I was aware of an unknown power; uncannily, instinctively I knew it was drawing closer. I paid extra-special attention to my aroused senses.

I saw Zalmné waiting for me. Something seemed different about him. I couldn't relate properly and was unable to figure it out. There was an unnatural barrier hindering our communication. It was most unusual! I put it out of my mind and blamed the ego for its non-stop interference.

I said, "Take me to meet the High Priest." We began to walk away from the pool. At that precise moment it dawned on me suddenly, intuitively and I blurted out, "I want to go back."

As we retreated towards the pool, I wasn't at all surprised at seeing Zalmné relaxing in the water. I was a little perplexed and asked, "Who was the other man?"

"I have been testing you," he replied candidly, "to see whether you would recognise a false guide?"

At the second attempt we went to seek the High Priest. Out of the misty shadows of the inner-space; a man appeared. He had long fine white hair, and a long wispy white beard. He was wearing a pale green heavy cotton robe. I asked in surprise, "Who are you?"

"I am that which you seek, the Master of Perception." he replied.

I said, "Will you give me a gift and tell me its meaning?"

He put a sword in my hands saying, "This is the Sword of Truth. It will slash the mystical veil. By it; your mortal sins will perish. By its power the secret knowledge will be revealed to you on your spiritual journey."

We returned to the pool and I relaxed in the cool clear water. It made me feel sleepy and tranquil. Explorations of the upper plane are always tiring, by bathing, I become restful.

Now I was aware the love for Zalmné had increased. In my heart I knew it to be a rare thing - so enchanting, uncomplicated and undemanding. I said farewell to my beloved Zalmné, and reunited with my semi-conscious body.

Time of meditation: 10.30 AM 5/10/90

19

THE TWINS - The Double Love

I walked towards the pool but did not see my Zalmné. Instead, a different Cherokee Indian greeted me. I stared at him blankly in astonishment and asked. "Where is Zalmné?" Pointing in the direction of the forest, he replied, "He will return soon."

Then I saw beloved Zalmné galloping towards us on his black stallion. His long straight hair was tied back platted in a single strand. He was wearing a thick fur shawl slung in a casual fashion over his bare skin. He commented, "We have to go on a journey to search for my friend's lost true love. We have to find her."

I sat with Zalmné on the bare-back of the stallion. The wind was cool, rushing across my face, whipping my hair. I held on tightly as he searched through every valley and vale. But alas, the girl was elusive and could not be found!

We returned to the pool-side and we saw a woman waiting. She said, "I have lost my love."

The man stepped forward and their love was once more united.

I asked for their gift and for its meaning.

The woman took off the necklace she was wearing; handing it to me, she said, "By wearing the gift I have given to you, you will be able to put into perspective the love which exists between you and your God."

I said farewell and walked away to the cave to be reunited with my still meditating body.

Time of meditation: 3.45 PM 8/10/90

THE CHARIOT - The Union

I had difficulty in visualising the inner world. It is not always easy to side-track the ego to obtain the inner-imagery. The ego refuses to recede into the background of the unconscious thereby the astral landscape is hazy; the perceptions are weak and blurry. It took me at least fifteen minutes of hard concentrated meditation before I succeeded in smashing the ego's blockage.

I found my Zalmné sitting cross-legged in a deep thought. Adopting a similar posture, I sat next to him; waiting for him to finish.

I was always happy to be with him. The calmness he exuded touched my spirit and made me feel immensely calm. My green dress was hung on a branch blowing in the breeze. I fetched it and wore it. Immediately, my senses became more alive.

Zalmné emerged from his inner-contemplation. I said, "I would like to see the Chariot."

He did not move from the pool-side as I looked; from the pool a woman appeared, bathed in a golden luminous light. I tried to bring her into focus but she was like a. ghostly spectre. At last she came into full view and I saw her very clearly.

She was standing elegant and erect like a Roman-statue. Then I saw approaching from behind her a chariot pulled by four white stallions. It stopped right in front of us. The woman's loveliness was beyond belief and difficult to describe!

Her hair was golden and her large topaz-blue eyes matched the blue-green chiffon gown she was wearing. Her skin was smooth and lustrous. I was mesmerised by her large clear eyes. They induced a fascinating and rapturous passion that seemed to well for her from the unfathomable depth of my being.

She came with us to the home of the Old Magician. Once there, he gave us permission to enter the Cave of Desire. The Chariot and I stepped inside. Zalmné waited just at the entrance, within reach; if I needed his assistance.

The Chariot said, "Please lie down. I will proceed to heal your other unconscious female desire. So that you are less aware of it and it disperses from your psyche altogether." She then touched my genital chakra with a healing crystal. I was conscious of heat flowing through the pelvic region.

I was thrilled to be united to an intangible source I had not even dreamed of. I remained quiet and thoughtful. In my own way, I accepted it as one of the lessons to be learnt from the inner-domain.

Zalmné and I returned to the pool. I lay down in the sparkling water to ease my body, which was still slightly tingling from the psychic lesson with the Chariot. When my equanimity had been restored sufficiently. I said farewell, and rejoined my physical body .

Time of meditation: 7.15 AM 12/10/90

THE STRENGTH - The Faith

I met my beloved Zalmné by the pool-side. He was his usual quiet contemplative self. He was wearing the traditional costume of the Cherokee Indian. His face and trunk painted in different colours and patterns. On his head he wore a glorious head-dress spreading out in a magnificent feathered-array. He looked astonishingly handsome and dignified.

He indicated that I should mount his stallion and sit behind him. I did as he commanded. The ego was trying its hardest to ruin the depth of my meditation field, and I was having trouble in concentrating on the inner- imagery again. With perseverance I defeated the rebellious interference of the ego's hold to keep me in the province of the physical world; and entered the domain of the astral world, through the meditation-state.

I said, "Take me to see the Strength." Instantly, we were surrounded by a mystical vision. A figure appeared wearing a white loose robe. I saw that the features were fresh, innocent and angel-like almost like a child. His wispy fair hair hanging loose touching the shoulders. His delightful, clear blue eyes were wide-open and smiling in merriment.

The figure came nearer and spoke. "I am The Spirit." I was a little bit surprised by these words. I asked for a gift and its meaning.

"I am giving you a precious gem," the Spirit said, " plucked from the Tree of Heaven. This I will lodge in your forehead. By its power, you will be in communion with the divine source. By its strength you will conquer the tribulations of the chosen path. From you I require that you observe all the Commandments, then you will find the wisdom you are searching for."

I was elated in the presence of the Spirit and was overwhelmed. I told Zalmné to soothe me. He caressed me with his gentle hands and poured cool water on my hot brow. My calm returned.

I retraced the path leading to the cave and rejoined with my still body.

Time of meditation: 12/10/90 PM

THE HERMIT - The Recluse

I contacted the inner world by my inward meditations but found it amazingly difficult to remain in the visual field. The images were fuzzy drifting in and out of focus. I moaned in frustration, "Sometimes I have a real problem in relating to this dimension!"

Zalmné explained, that it was my ego, saying, "It puts up barriers between the two dimensions. It is struggling with the real and the false. It is dumbfounded by the sensations it has to assimilate of the different spheres. It has to transfigure the negative and positive realities. It keeps pulling you back to the reality of the physical world; where it is safe; cacooned in the mortal flesh. It will delude you and will destroy the inner vision, if you let it. But with practised self-control, you can be rid of its grand delusion, and be in touch with your real self."

He advised me to wear the green dress to help me relate better to the dimensional-depth. I fetched it off the branch and wore it. Immediately, my senses became more vibrant. I was elated and giddy with exuberance. We danced around twirling with happiness on the silken waters of the pool.

At this point I must explain, there is no limit to what one can achieve on this plane. Every wish is possible and granted. Life is not cumbersome as it is on earth. Here, the vibrations are light. One glides over the distances; transporting in an instant from one dimension to next. When I use the word 'walking' in the text; I literally mean we are floating across the astral expanse.

I asked to see the Hermit. Instantaneously, like an illusionist he produced a canoe upon the water. We stepped in and journeyed along the river's course

22

until we came to a small clearing in the dense part of the forest; where we stopped and got out.

It was then I noticed the old straw hut. There were no windows in it; and only a small square exit. We stepped inside to look. It was dark and cool. On a. hard wooden box the Hermit sat with his eyes closed. His hair was white and unkempt; his face pale and sallow, the skin paper-like, drawn and wrinkled. He seemed to be content in his sparse surroundings. I asked him emphasising my question, "Why do you sit like this?"

"This is my judgement, " the Hermit said. "This is my only life and I have been sitting here forever. I do not know of any other-way to live. But as you are the seeker of the spiritual path; and as you seek me, I will not turn you away. As you can see, I am free of every painful worldly manifestation. I have forsaken my material life for the sake of the spiritual.. I am the recluse who has merged his soul with God."

After his wise counsel, I was elated. Then I asked for his gift and its significance.

"Take this twig out of my hand," he offered. "When you feel lonely in your mortal world look at it; and remember my plight. This way, you will alleviate your loneliness. From you all I need in return is that you are humble, without any pride, vanity or stubbornness. When you have fulfilled these things within yourself, your life will be much enriched and rewarding."

I must admit I have learnt a lot from the wise words of the Hermit. I am in awe of his sagacious wisdom.

He returned to the pool where I said farewell and came back via the cave to my meditating body.

Time of meditation: 10-15 PM 13/10/90

WHEEL OF FORTUNE - The Wealth

Today, I experienced much difficulty in remaining in the inner world. The perception and connection was weak disintegrating in the meditating mind. The ego, gripped tight with full maximum force; only with determined effort and powerful concentration, was I able to be free of its invisible net. Eventually I was, floating across the iridescent astral-space.

I saw Zalmné sitting on his stallion. The sight of him pleased my senses. I was very much aware of his magnetism as I moved closer. We conversed by thought-transference. "Take me to the Wheel of Fortune." I requested.

He pulled me up to be beside him. We trekked gingerly through the forest. I could feel his rhythmic muscles rippling under my touch. Finally, he stopped at a tranquil beach and we dismounted.

I searched the horizon and in the distance I could just see the 'Wheel of Fortune'. It came trundling towards us and stopped. I asked it to change

23

into a. human form but it did not co-operate. I asked again but it still resisted my demand. I wondered how one could talk to a wheel?

It looked like an ordinary bicycle wheel only stronger and thicker around its circumference and heavier. I asked for the third time, but with stubbornness it denied my request. In the end I gave up! Suddenly, it spoke. "I will not transform until you have learned the real wisdom of wealth."

"I don't know what you are telling me exactly." I said, "Can you explain more fully?"

"Fine." it said, "Let's go and find the Justice. He will be able to solve our problem." I resolved to search for him on my return.

Time of meditation: 9.15 AM 14/10/90

THE JUSTICE - The Judgement

I had absolutely no trouble in locating the Justice. He was as clear as daylight and I saw him instantly.

He was the judge of the inner world. He wore a. long black gown and a white wig like in the physical world. He gave judgement to all the archetypes.

We stepped inside the court. All the archetypes assembled for this hearing, except the recluse, the Hermit. The Justice gave permission to the Wheel of Fortune to begin:

"I will not harmonise with this person from the exterior world, until she fully realises the real value of wealth. She has no definite comprehension of fortune. In all her worldly living she craves for money. Gold has been her consuming passion. She chases wealth with fervour. When she can renounce her greed, then I will deal with her. When she has removed the god of wealth from within her heart, then I will give her my counsel. Until then, I refuse to communicate with her." said the Wheel of fortune.

The Justice approved of the Wheel of Fortune's decision. All the other archetypes cheered and clapped in agreement.

"We will assemble again in this court at a later date when this lady has found her wisdom." said the Justice. With a wave of his hand, he dismissed the ensemble present.

After everyone left, I asked for his gift and its meaning.

He replied, "I am giving you a miniature pair of scales. Weigh your actions on it everyday. Put your bad deeds on the left and the good ones on the right. Endeavour to tip the scales to the right; this way, you will weigh your 'true moments of happiness'. You will harmonise and be in concordance with everything around you."

Zalmné and I returned to the pool. I was quietly reflecting on the wise words of the Justice and Wheel of Fortune. We contemplated for a while;

24

as it has become customary to inner-meditate within the meditation. Then I said farewell and rejoined my body.

Time of meditation: 9-15 PM 14/10/90

THE HANGED MAN - The Four Rivers

I went to the pool. I realised the ego was quiet, submerged in the domain of the unconscious; completely calm, totally unresisting.

The inner world when it focused was limpid, lucent and lucid. When I found Zalmné, he was quiet and contemplating. He was sitting in a yoga-fashion; staring as if mesmerised by dark unfathomable depths. I adopted the same repose and attitude and joined him in the inner-meditation.

When finally we finished our fervent contemplation; he stood up. I noticed he was twiddling with a short piece of rope. I wasn't too surprised, he must have known, I wanted to visit the Hanged Man.

My love for him is now complete. I have never known this kind of loving it is intrepid and incomprehensible. I have surrendered to it in the totality of its existence. He interrupted my thoughts.

"I have made you a hammock between the trees. Take a short rest and relax before we proceed." I lay down and stared at the blue sky, the rhythm was soothing. The sun's warmth washed over me, and I became tranquil and sleepy. Then an inner vision gripped me by its mysterious power.

I talked to the Sun and asked it to transform into human form. The Sun granted my wish, and I saw Archangel Gabriel appear in the inner-space. He was huge; his head touched the top-most clouds; his massive wings covered the whole expanse of the sky. Many radiant rainbows arched above his head and his golden aura shone through a misty white haze.

The emerald light was throbbing in my third eye and then I perceived the great vision.

Corpses were hanging on the trees in the woodland. Goblins were discarding the carcasses into the four rivers. I exclaimed, "What's happening?" Archangel Gabriel replied; "We are in the Land of the Hanged Men, their bodies will be thrown into the rivers; and their souls will be carried to the appointed places, according to the deeds they have performed in their mortal life. They will traverse through the four rivers; of honey, wine, blood and salt. In the river of honey, there will be no sorrow. In the river of wine, they shall forever be intoxicated. In the river of blood, many tears will fall; and lastly; in the river of salt, there will be much pain."

This powerful vision dispersed and another followed. I was inspired:-

There is a silver moon,
In the silver sky,
And a single star shining brightly.

25

Mary was divine in the silver light,
Baby Jesus asleep in her arms,
So innocent in her motherly hold.

I communicated with Lady Mary. "The silver wand you thrust between my eyes has completely obliterated my blindness. My eyes have opened. I am able to perceive more which is hidden." She did not say anything. Instead, she just smiled. Her serene eyes touched the depth of my soul.

We returned to the pool. I relaxed for a while, then I said farewell, and walked towards the cave whereupon I rejoined with my meditating body.

Date of meditation: 19/10/90

TEMPERANCE - The Time

I was standing beside the pool; and today the inner-perceptions flowed effortlessly easily in the astral-dimension.

Zalmné was near the water; sitting yoga-fashion contemplating in repose. As I approached him; I could see his countenance was stern, sullen and sedate I could read nothing.

His hair was platted in one single strand and he was dressed in the traditional costume of the Cherokee Indian.

I sat down in front of him; held his hands in mine and expressed my great love for him. I felt his calm gaze upon my face, our awareness was total, complete, without any flaws. There were no hidden depths or profound meanings. It was so strong, tears of elation welled in my heart.

After I had recovered sufficiently from this thought-provoking love, I asked him to take me to see the Temperance.

He summoned his white-winged stallion. It obediently responded to his call. We flew in the sky and as we passed over the land of the Magician, I saw the lamp of knowledge burning brightly. The Magician joined us in the search, looking everywhere, but the Temperance remained elusive.

We were just about to abandon the search when Temperance casually sauntered out of the woods. He looked like an ancient monk, dressed in black robes with a large hood over his face. As he came nearer I saw he was devoid of any flesh. On his skeletal-form; dry flaky skin hung loose. Large maggots wriggled in the mouth-cavity, and infectious sores and yellow pus mutilated his body. It was pitiful to see.

Zalmné commented, "This is Temperance."

In shock I asked, "Why do you exist in such a terrible state?"

Temperance replied, "I was not temperate in all my actions and this is my punishment. I am as a living death. When I am honest and just, and have learnt to curb all my insatiable desires. When I have cleansed my heart of all the aggressions of the past, present and the future, only then will I become

26

TEMPERANCE

THE WORLD

once more a true human being."

I asked for his gift and its purpose.

"I am giving you a root from the great oak that has stood the test of time in dignity. It sees all, hears all and says nothing. I am putting it in your right thigh. It will give you much sustenance, patience and temperance. The great oak has borne many seeds and scattered them over the land. I want you to retain the wisdom learnt of this experience. Search the depth and breadth of it within your heart, and be temperate with all that you deal with. Weather the storms in severe conditions. Have faith and strength and nothing will fail you. Everything is within your grasp. Be brave and have courage. When the way ahead is dark, let the light of the emerald guide you. If you observe the judgement of temperance; you will store its great knowledge within your heart."

The Temperance then left us and walked back in to the woods.

I needed time to reflect: This was a lesson I had not expected.

We went to visit the Star-Alien as I liked to be with him. He was waiting for us on the calm eastern shore. We stepped inside the crystal cubicle and were airborne. Once more I was inspired:-

> The Star-Alien made love to me,
> On the shores of Azizi.
> It was a dream I could not comprehend;
> The stars were whizzing around me,
> The whole of my self,
> United and ignited with the Universe.

We returned to the pool. I saw the two black mambas swimming in the water. My Zalmné remarked, "The kundalini is beginning to awaken within you."

I rested for a while before returning to my worldly body. He sensed; I did not want to leave and offered to walk with me to the cave. He said farewell in the dim shadowy light and once more, I was aware of being united with my physical form.

Date of meditation: 28/10/90

THE TOWER - The Holy Grail

The inner world had become easier to locate; it is clear and bright. I did not experience any difficulty from the ego. Zalmné was waiting for me. He was quiet and cheerful, which was rather surprising! I don't very often find him in this sort of mood. Nevertheless, I remained silent and did not make a comment.

I noticed he was dressed once more in his traditional Cherokee clothes. He wore the full-feathered head-dress and had painted his chest and face. Even after all our time together, his face remains obscure and I am not able to describe his features. I can recall his masculine form and his clothing, but not his features.

The fire was burning a bright orange and crackling loudly; and the white stallion was grazing peacefully. I was hypnotised by the leaping flames and the sound of the cracking seemed like distant thunder. I was unaware of Zalmné standing in a circle of scorpions and when I looked again they weren't threatening! Zalmné remarked, "Don't be afraid, they will not harm me."

I said, "I want to see the Tower." We sat astride his white stallion and it galloped into the forest. Zalmné explained, "We will fly above the earth's magnetic field - there will be less interference on that plane especially from the ego." It was electrifying in the timeless zone. I held on tightly as we flew past time and space.

In the vast expanse of white time I saw a reservoir full of clear sparkling water. To the right stood a Tower. Standing on the top turret was a man. He was in his late thirties, quite handsome, with black curly hair and a beard.

I asked in surprise, "Who are you?" I was taken aback by his reply, "I am King Arthur."

I asked for his gift and its meaning,

"I am putting in your right eye a pale blue-green topaz," he offered. "Its light will direct you to a secret passage. The meaning of life will be revealed. You are at this moment standing on the Holy Grail. What I need from you is that you learn from this experience and learn to assimilate the mysteries as they are shown. I will now take you through the tunnel of fire."

Two great wooden doors opened and yellow, gold and violet flames leapt around us. It engulfed us and my soul caught fire; like flotsam we drifted towards the heavens. All heavenly bodies became alive before my eyes.

I perceived creation in motion. Time disintegrated and space and matter collapsed and a. great tide of waters formed. I heard my Zalmné saying, "We are floating in the waters of the heavens." Then I saw the pulsating white light contained in a vessel of pure crystal diamonds. The vessel was placed on the table of offering. Zalmné explained, "The white light pulsates in the worlds and the heavens."

Bathed in the brightness of the white light I perceived the Father and the Holy Spirit; the mighty Angels and the great Prophets. The face of God was still hidden, the mystical veil was impenetrable; shrouded in an unfathomable Mystery. Zalmné continued to explain. "You will not see his face until you are ready to comprehend it; and you are prepared to be with him at all times."

The whole essence was pure and mystifying; such great power and knowledge was present on this plane. The white light made me feel drowsy and blissful. I did not want to leave! I was totally submerged in its mesmerising beauty.

Zalmné spoke again. "When the white light stops radiating and the vessel ceases to pulsate, then the many worlds and heavens will recede back to the darkness. Everything will return to eternity. The ones who will survive are the seekers of the holy path."

We returned to the pool. I found that I was still plugged to the sheer intensity of the upper experience.

Zalmné was sympathetic, he obliged, "Go and rest in the hammock to be soothed and calmed." I lay down and relaxed. After a further deep search, I left the inner plane to be reunited with my physical form.

Date of meditation: 3/11/90 8.00 AM.

THE MOON - The Dream

I walked towards the pool but did not glimpse beloved Zalmné. Instead a man I had never seen before stood by the water. At first glance I noticed his magnificent turban and that he was superbly dressed. He was standing perfectly still, as if mesmerised by water, harmonising with its mystery.

I wondered why he was here, but dared not ask. I thought it wise not to.

I searched for my Zalmné and found him leaning against a tree merging with the opaque shadows. My green dress was blowing in the wind. I fetched it and put it on. The twilight was beginning to fall; dusky hues hidden within its beauteous depths.

By this time the strange person had vanished. Zalmné and I stood together holding hands. The full moon shone effulgent in the dark cloak of the night. The silver light enchanting.

I asked the Moon, to become a humanoid. And out of the rhythmic movements of the pink and purple shadowy twilight, a boat emerged. In it I saw a lovely woman. I held my breath in wonder. I was entranced by her beauty. Her hair falling to her ankles, straight and silky; the colour of silver-platinum glistening in the moon-light. Her lively blue eyes were bright and beautiful, sparkling like sapphires. Her complexion was soft and smooth. She wore a. shimmering semi-transparent gown in a creamy-white flimsy silk; and myriad precious jewels adorned it like fluorescent fireflies in the dark. Her translucent gossamer wings were embellished with white lustrous pearls glimmering in the darkness. She came near to me and spoke. "I am the Lady of the Moon and I live in its waters."

Straightaway I asked, "Can you give me the gift and tell me its meaning?"

"I have here a moon-gem which I will put in your crown chakra. One half is pink and the other half is a pale lilac. When you have absorbed these colours within you, a wondrous mystery will awaken inside you. This will be attainable and in your grasp on the intersection of earthly-spiritual domain. With your consciousness now fully opened, any hesitation you harboured will disappear."

Taking hold of my hand she said, "Come with me. I will take you further along your path."

She guided me into the boat and we crossed over to the other side of the pool. As we stepped out, I saw the Star-Alien. The atmosphere was charged. No one spoke. A weird feeling seemed to be flowing between us, evoking wonderful sensation. The ecstasy overwhelming to the point of a spiritual release, immensely satisfying. I was flying somewhere in the heavens and the friendliness of the Moon-goddess and Star-Man was perfectly delightful and tangible.

After this I retraced my steps to the other side. Zalmné was waiting. I said, " I saw a cobra. What did that mean?"

He explained, "You have been touched by the kundalini. Now it will be your companion on the chosen path, and guide you with its esoteric wisdom. You will amass its knowledge."

Before I rejoined my physical body, the Old Magician filled my psyche. Then I met the Fool; his light shone in my dark mind, enabling me grasp the truth. Shortly after I visited the High Priestess; her pure love transferred to my heart. Next, the Sun gave me a profuse, warm blessing. They all knew my steps on the spiritual-path and guided me on my inner-journey towards my final destination. I said farewell to everyone present and returned to the cave and then to my own body.

Date of meditation: 23/11/90

THE LAST JUDGEMENT - The Revelation

Zalmné was waiting for me at the pool. He was dressed in a dark-brown buffalo-skin. He had parted his hair in the middle and platted it in one strand. Around his head he wore the white headband adorned with two dove feathers. Lodged in the cavity of his shoulder-blades against his spine lay a long leather pouch containing his bow and arrows. As he came nearer I sensed his mood to be light and cheerful. I said, "Take me to the Last Judgement."

He pointed upwards and remarked, "I will shoot the arrow into the sky to bring down the Book of Judgement." He pulled the bow-string and released the arrow and it spiralled upwards to the unknown. The great book floated down held in the hands of Lord Gabriel. He spoke to me saying, "I hold in my hands, The Book of Divine Power. God is, always and will be. He has no beginning and no ending. He is free from time and forever eternal. By His wisdom alone the worlds have been created; God's people can share in His infinite love. They are invited unto His Heavens to be in His Kingdom forever."

From the far distance I heard the voice of God speaking to me, "I have woken from my eternal sleep. Those of you who believe in Me shall see the Light of my Soul." Then I saw a mighty vision. An electric storm slashed the Heavens, blue-lightning flashed and forked in every part of the earth. The battle between Lucifer and Lord Michael began! The Revelations unfolded before my very eyes. Finally the Great Dragon was unleashed and the Destruction devoured the magnificent world.

We descended to the pool. I asked Lord Gabriel for his gift and its purpose.

"I am giving you an apple from the Tree of life. One half of it, I will put in your larynx. When you have digested its juice, you will become intoxicated by the sweet nectar of belief. Your sorrow will end and you will become entangled in the Divine Love."

He continued, "I will place the other half of the apple in the cavity of your heart. Its psychic force will make your transition easier and smoother. In exchange, you must observe all the Commandments. The apple's power will help you become adept at giving and receiving love. Live in peace and harmony and make your existence a happy dwelling place in the lands of the earth." Then he ascended upwards to the heavens.

I stayed with beloved Zalmné for a while relaxing after the experience before saying farewell and rejoining my mortal body.

Date of meditation: 27/11/90

SPHERE OF MALKUTH

MY CAREFREE YOUTH

I met Zalmné beside the pool. It had been very difficult to break the ego's barrier. It kept me tied up with the worldly swirling mind-thoughts and realities. With focused attention and concentration, I succeeded in entering the meditation-space.

I spoke to Zalmné and commented lightly, "I have not visited the astral world for a few days as the previous trip to the Last Judgement somewhat depressed me." I waited for his answer.

"Your ego is being transformed. Its worldly reality is gradually dissolving from your psyche. It will put up barricades across the path of your progress." He continued, "Come with me I will show you the truth." Hands clasped tightly we walked to the White Temple. We meditated in front of the light. The burning candle cast golden shadows on the Altar. Zalmné commented, "This is the eternal flame of love - it will never extinguish."

"Tell me," I said, "I am seeking the meaning of true happiness? Does it exist?"

"It is very elusive." he replied, "The pleasure we experience is an illusion. We are deluding ourselves. The joy of earthly life is brief compared to the immortality of spiritual love."

Then I questioned him about something that had been lurking in my mind for a long time. "Who is God?"

"He is the light of our world. He is the matter, living, dead and the unknown. He is in your heart, in mine and in the skies. He lives and breathes within everything."

"Then who is Lucifer?"

"He lives in the Garden of Time as the Snake. The garden where life was born."

"Am I now ready to climb the Tree of life?"

There was total silence. No answer from him! I asked three times before he responded! "Cast your mind back to when you were eight. You climbed that apple tree to the top; even so, you were afraid. Nevertheless, you went ahead and when you looked down from the top you were frightened, although it was exhilarating being there. From its highest point you saw many things, which would not have been possible from the ground. I will tell you to go ahead and explore. Eat of the ripe fruits of wisdom and pick only those that are sweet in goodness."

For a brief spell in the meditation - we went back to my carefree youth. I could once again see the hazy golden sun ablaze with crimson fire on the horizon. The huge water-melons ripe and round. The mud dried hard, cracked like clay. I walked on the white bridge from Kholvad to Katour. The snaking river flowing underneath. I traversed the fields of my youth, free as the wind and the bird. I was at rest with nature and God. My Spirit was calm like the water.

When we returned to the pool-side I felt fulfilled. I did not want to leave the inner world. I wanted to remain here forever. Zalmné broke my reverie.

"Go back now your other world is waiting for you."

Date of meditation: 7/12/90

VEIL OF THE LESSER MYSTERIES

THE DEEPER MYSTERY

I went to the pool. Zalmné was sitting In a yoga position totally reposed in contemplation. There was an adder beside him. I was not afraid. I have become used to seeing the snakes in the inner dimension. After he emerged from his own personal deep search, I mentioned the empty, listless loneliness. I was feeling and asked what could be done about it.

"Go and put on your green dress then we will go and ask the Hermit for his advice."

He rowed the long narrow canoe and arriving at the clearing we went inside the Hermit's straw hut. He still sat on his wooden-box. I held both his hands and gently questioned. "How can you sit alone like this? My loneliness is nothing compared to yours, yet, I feel the weight of it bearing down on me."

He replied just as gently. "Let us go and visit the Justice. He will clarify our situation." We went to the inner court and there on the golden scales, he weighed our lonely moments. Mine hardly tipped the scales compared to the Hermit's and I was truly ashamed. I vowed never to feel lonely again.

When we came back to the pool, I glimpsed briefly, the Moon-goddess and the Star-Man on the opposite bank. This time, though, I only waved and did not wander across to join them.

I confided to my Zalmné. "There is something else I wish to ask. It is gnawing in my unconscious like a stone grinding in the mill. It is the question of death. What is it?"

"Death is a phase we have to pass through, after it life begins anew. It is only a barrier between the two realities."

I blurted out, "Is there a Deeper Mystery?"

"Let us go and see the High Priestess - she will answer your question." We were transported instantly to her realm. She came again as the Lady Mary - the baby asleep in her arms.

I said, "You gave me the silver wand to see my way on the path. I have seen many things but the one that eludes me is the Mystery."

She placed two golden lights at each end of the psychic wand. Immediately, I became giddy with exuberance. The inner sphere was yielding and luminescent.

"Come with me, I will show you." She said.

We climbed to the top of her crystalline cave, went inside a short secret tunnel and stepped out onto the 'Land of Freedom'.

She continued, "What you seek will be here. No death, no pain and no fear. The climate is temperate and all the pleasures will be provided bountifully. This is where true joy begins. Take a fragment of this setting and put it in your heart, then you will be attuned to the Mystery. You will hear the Song of Heaven and the secret of Life will be revealed."

After this revelation I went inside the Inner Temple to pray. I prayed to the

Lord God within me and outside of me this day and for ever-more and for eternal life.

Then I said farewell to my beloved guide and rejoined my mortal body.

Date of meditation: 13/1/91

THE TREE OF LIFE

I met Zalmné by the pool. He was wearing his white silk tunic, headband and two dove feathers. As soon as I saw him I said, "For some time now, I have wondered whether you are my real guide?"

"Yes." He answered promptly. Then I tried to visualise his face in my mind's eye, but I saw only a blur where his features should be. I placed both my hands on his face. His jaw-line felt angular, eyebrows thick and nose straight and pointed.

"I have come to ask your guidance on the Qabalistic Tree. The last time I attempted to seek its wisdom, I failed miserably. I realised my ego and my psyche were unable to grasp the knowledge."

He took my hand and we went to the base of the tree. "This is the beginning where you begin." he said, "As you move up the tree of life you will encounter the various Aspects of God. He is the living force of the tree. The middle part of it represents the solar plexus of God, where creation lives and dies, and is again created and lives and dies again over and over. The ten working forces of God which sustain the tree of life are the foundations of living truth. God himself is the Food of the tree of life. It takes the nourishment of God as its life source and Life flows from it."

I asked, "Is it possible to see God?"

"You will not see God with your eyes but you will perceive Him with your other senses. He is all the things you wish Him to be for He is like the chameleon. He is able to change shape and form."

He explained that on the astral plane the Holy Spirit cloaks those it touches with a pure brilliant light.

I was elated and overwhelmed by his wise words.and returned to the White Temple to pray. The Flame of Love burned brightly on the altar. In my contemplation I was with my God.

Whilst we had been exploring the form of God; the twenty-two archetypes had held a special meeting. I asked; why. Zalmné explained, "The twenty-two archetypes are the aspects of God. They are the connections between the Earth and God. They are the channels from which his energy flows; transferring from God to Man and from Man to God. The tree of life is the food of these energies. Its vitality which keeps the Flame of Life lit for ever."

I must have been in a rush to write it down; for I returned rather hastily to my barely-breathing body sitting deeply in meditation.

Date of meditation: 31/1/91

THE FLIGHT OF THE SERPENT

I tried to reach Zalmné at the Autumn pool; but the inner-images were hazy. I travelled deeper into the meditation-field; hoping to lose track of the persistent devilish ego. I smashed the ego's presence and entered the mind-space, and eventually with intense concentration, I was in the inner world.

I saw Zalmné sitting bare-back on his white stallion wearing his glorious multi-feathered head-dress. On his chest he had inscribed the kundalini serpent. His whole body was adorned with many weird mystical symbols and on his long smooth legs he had drawn eagles and scorpions. In his right hand he held a miniature totem pole, carved with images of dancing Shamans.

Whilst contemplating on the mysticism he portrayed. I felt light tingling sensation, surge through me; shocking and awakening the kundalini into action: It stirred and moved in my belly, travelling upwards to my mouth and nostrils, to my eyes and ears. Its head snaked forward towards my crown piercing it before dividing into many smaller serpents.. I was the Medusa.

I suppressed my ego and I was aware of flying through an unknown dimension. My spirit moved out of my astral body from the crown and in this state of consciousness I was intensely aware of God. I reunited with my astral body coming back through the third-eye, sensing that this experience had cleansed and transformed all my chakra centres. I had been close to a mystical being. Zalmné warned, "Don't ever take such perilous journeys alone! You may never return!" I said farewell and rejoined with my worldly body.

Date of meditation: 17/2/91

THE HOLY PATH

I did not see Zalmné at the pool, so I stepped inside the White Temple to pray. As I entered the dim light I saw him kneeling beside the altar in fervent contemplation, so I joined him in deep reflection.

I had a distinct feeling we were not alone; someone was in our midst. Then I opened my eyes and saw a man standing serenely behind the flickering flame. He was stoutly built; broad-shouldered and big-boned. He had a long bushy-beard and bright smiling eyes. He was wearing a long cream-coloured robe which spread out on the floor and trailed behind him.

Zalmné commented. "He is the great sage - The guardian of the holy path." He let us pass and we ascended a white marble stairway all the way up to the gates of heaven.

Zalmné continued, "We are on the holy path- I will accompany you to the top, but from there on you must go alone. No guide or spirit is allowed to go with you. The knowledge must be yours alone."

I was afraid. I did not want him to leave me at the top of the stairway. In great distress and trepidation I walked further on, into the land of the unknown. In it I saw a massive empty throne studded with many precious gems. A huge dazzling diamond lit the whole expanse with its heavenly glow.

In intrinsic fear I approached the throne; and then I sensed God. His invisibility cloaked me and I heard the words, "Sit down." I sat in it and the splendour of divine Love surrounded me and I was captivated.

The whole kaleidoscope of creation swirled around me and I discerned God's grace and humility, together with all the joy and suffering contained in His great heart. The tears of elation rolled down my cheeks.
I returned to the top of the stairway where Zalmné was waiting for me.

"How was it?" he enquired.

In total wonder I answered, "His holiness is gentle llike the soft winds drifting on a dreamy summers day."

Date of meditation: 21/2/91

THE WORLD

I went to our usual meeting place. I found Zalmné sitting in a long narrow canoe. "Get in." he said. The connection of the inner world was weak; and the inner-images kept drifting in and out of the my meditating mind. I could not see properly but I was intensely aware of his presence.

He commented, "We are going to find the World. Go and put on your green dress; the perceptions will become strong and you will see better." I did and immediately the mistiness of the inner world cleared.

We paddled the canoe. The river was frothy and turbulent. Its hissing effervescent waters tossed us. Then, suddenly; it stilled. I looked along the bank and saw a black stallion. Seated on it was a man of the medieval era, attired in a suit of armour.

"Who are you?" I questioned in surprise.

"I am Sir Lancelot." he answered.

"What is the gift you are offering and its purpose?" I asked.

"I will put on your left knee a tiny amount of debris collected from a black hole. By the weight, you will realise the density of matter."

His words inspired me:

> Man destroys the wondrous beauty of the world,
> The deep-blue sky and the lush-green land,
> An earthly paradise for man and woman,

As earth on Heaven.
Bird and beast dwell in tranquillity,
Fish and fowl of the splendid sea.
We returned to the pool. My heart stricken with grief, remorseful and sad.
I said farewell, found the cave and rejoined with my physical body.

Date of meditation: 10/3/91

THE RETURNING

I had not visited the astral-sphere for a few weeks. The last trip was depressing. I became despondent and lethargic. Also, the relationship I was involved in had distracted my attention away from the meditation. I had followed him abroad but the involvement failed miserably. Gripped in the throes of the critical, I turned once more to the meditation.

I returned to the familiar scene at the pool and waited for my Zalmné to appear. My green dress was still blowing in the wind. I put it on. It seemed nothing had changed. I was a little bit sad.

I sat on the grassy-verge, waiting. I looked into the depth of the transparent pool and to my utter surprise and astonishment saw Zalmné sitting completely submerged, fully clothed in total relaxation! I must have disturbed him in his contemplation; for he opened his eyes. When he saw me, he gently pulled me in to sit beside him under the water.

We sat in the watery-depths for a long time. I was not the least bit afraid. Something odd had overtaken me. I was able to sit submerged in the fathoms and not drown. My senses were wholly alive, and I revelled in the pleasure; so pleasant and satisfying. I watched the spectacular fish-life floating by in slow motion. I thought, I am in harmony with God.

After the inner-search we strolled leisurely in the forest. We looked for the High Priestess but did not find her; so we relaxed on a huge yellow water-lily and bathed in the silver-bright water.

It dawned on me, everything was the same. All the love for my Zalmné was still there. Time had not worn away the goodness and sweetness of it; as is often the case, in physical life.

I was happy to be reunited with the mysterious element of the inner dimension.

I said farewell to my Zalmné and returned to my physical body.

Date of meditation: 30/5/91

THE ETERNAL

I walked on the familiar ground, and as I neared the pool I noticed beloved Zalmné sat in a yoga posture in calm relaxation. My green dress was blown by the inner-wind. I fetched it and put it on. I sat down facing him and took his hands in mine. Trying to figure out I questioned him,"Why have I not been able to see your face? Why?"

He replied in a short concise sentence. "It is for the best."

In my dreams I imagined him to be truly handsome. I thought, perhaps if I were to see him clearly, his beauty would blind me.

For a long time we sat silently in repose. It has become customary to meditate on the aspects of the inner-self. We do not talk as such; only the transfer of feeling is required for the transmission of communication. We understand each other in depth and are in perfect harmony, and in our solitude, we are seeking our God. The pleasure, widening, expanding to all parts of our being.

When the inner-meditation was over I said, "There are several things on my mind I want to discuss. I am profoundly alienated! The bridge between the inner and outer realities was extremely difficult to cross. My personal life is in a mess and somewhat chaotic! Mostly due to my lack of insight. To top it all, the I Ching predicted a 'Critical Mass' phase: What am I to do?" I wailed in distress.

Zalmné did not offer a solution; instead he was kind and understanding, as though, sharing my difficulties.

We turned towards the pool. The sun shone on the water reflecting light and shade. All of a sudden it turned black and a dark tunnel formed in the middle. "Come," commanded Zalmné.

"Where are we going?" I asked perplexed and slightly alarmed!

"Let us step in the corridors of time," he replied.

We levitated fast in the dark and rocky earth. It seemed we were travelling to the core. But then we changed direction and the light became misty and semi-transparent.

I looked back. The clear blue skies and pearly white clouds gradually receded into the distance.

We were going, through a translucent corridor in space enclosed inside a circular transparent bubble, travelling fast in the time-space continuum.

Zalmné spoke, "Man has tremendous power - his knowledge is vast. One day soon, he will travel at the speed of light. Spaceships will become obsolete. He will create corridors in space and vibrate through them in an instant. He will explore all the planets; not only in this galaxy, but also the myriad others. Man will comprehend matter. It will dissolve at his touch and become solute so that limitless dimensions are reachable. Man is akin to God. He can attain powers; if used wisely they will benefit him. If used wrongly; they will eventually to destroy him. To God; the world is a toy. Time means nothing and space is tangible."

His words inspired me:

> God does not sleep,
> For He is eternally awake.
> He does not eat,
> For He is always full.
> He never dies,
> For death never takes Him.
> He never needs pleasure,
> For He is the blissful state.

Zalmné spoke again, "I am taking you on an eternal journey. I want you to realise the kingdom is great. The pleasure we receive from the world is not comparable to the blissful state of God. If He so wished, a trillion galaxies would collapse at His command. He is the eternal life, fluctuating in the dark wilderness of cognition."

He continued, "Our existence on earth is temporary; as matter is meant to decompose. Man cannot control matter, although he trying very hard to do so. Its destiny lies in the hands of God. This life is a trial for man; so that he becomes self-realised, almost akin to God himself."

He carried on expounding, "Man is on the spiritual-road at this moment in time. He is becoming awake and has the ability to raise himself to the higher throne. God eternally waits for man; so that he can join Him in his kingdom and share all the pleasures available to him through his senses. By endeavour on the spiritual road, he will find the kingdom which exists for him on the higher planes of living. Man will never become God; as has been prophesied by various unethical sources but will reside with Him in spirit; sharing the fruit of divine wisdom. God is the Supreme, the Ultimate, the Divinity and the Bliss. His Spirit roams free, and for all those souls who want to be united with him, He shall be theirs. When one has reached this blissful plane, death will never visit with its immense pain. Eternal living therefore is supreme bliss."

I thanked Zalmné for taking me on the eternal journey. I said, "I must return immediately to write; otherwise, the momentous experience will recede back into the unconscious. All the wisdom learnt will be lost and devoured in the confusion of the intellect. The ego takes over and controls my body; and when I return, all the clarity of knowledge becomes murky: As the ego cannot accept the knowledge I have acquired."

This particular time I really did not want to leave the inner world. I wanted to stay with my beloved Zalmné. He said gently, "You must go now." I said farewell and came back to the material world.

Date of meditation: 9/6/91

MYSTICISM OF THE DIVINE SOURCE

DESTINY

I have now adapted a new technique of entering the inner world by contacting Pisces and Aquarius at the Autumn pool. I begin my meditation and immediately I am transported to our usual place; on the opposite bank of the pool. This particular time was most unusual to say the least. The meeting proceeded extraordinarily; levitating and floating in the air about six feet off the ground. Afterwards I crossed over to Zalmné, who always waits for me, whilst I am in unity with the Moon-goddess and Star-Man.

I addressed him, "Could you arrange a special meeting with the archetypes?" He nodded his head in agreement, and sent out a silent call across the expanse of the inner-world. One by one, they came out of their abodes to the gathering by the pool.

I perceived Death to be outstanding and impressive. He sat erect on his black stallion, proud and arrogant, dressed wholly in black. His eyes glowered through the small slit-openings.

The High Priestess looked psychic and supernatural. She came in a carriage made from dazzling-blue crystal.

The Hermit joined this special meeting. This is the only journey he has ever taken from his straw hut. He came in a boat of translucent-white crystal.

All the Archetypes assembled by the pool; leaving for a while their abodes scattered about in the space of the inner world. They formed a circle around the White Temple. The Justice presiding as the judge. I asked them all for judgement on my worldly actions and the way I had lived my life, and what was my destiny.

The Justice spoke, "We cannot proffer any assistance, guidance or information on the question of Destiny. We are your individual archetypes who guide destiny on its way. We do not issue commands. That comes from the higher quarters. Basically, you are your own judge. Within you and outside of you are governing elements which take you through the bewildering maze of life. We exist to help, nourish and strengthen you. We cannot directly answer questions on morality of good and evil. Our instructions are issued from the higher sources and then second by second, we set in motion the ticking of life's clock."

At this point I was inspired:-

> In my vision I saw,
> A young radiant princess,
> Dressed wholly in white.
> She cupped in her fragile hands,
> The chalice of eternal youth,

From which God's Creation poured.
All the archetypes left one by one, returning, to their homes. I said farewell to my beloved Zalmné and came back to my home, the world.

Date of meditation: 26/6/91

A DIFFERENT PATHWAY

I have now been with my guide for just over nine months. I think I am experiencing interference from the ego. I am very much aware of the impact on my body systems. It keeps hammering in my brain. The knowledge of the inner world cannot go on and on. It has to end. For some time it has lurked in my unconscious. Now it presents itself in my conscious mind and I ask myself is there an end to knowledge, or does the ocean go on forever? I think I am experiencing ego-death and it is testing me by erecting barriers to my progress.

There has been a tremendous upheaval in my personal life since February. I was very much involved in a relationship and the meditation had been filed and stored in the subconscious memory, to be resumed at a later date.

I have not meditated much since that time.

Recently, I have been introduced to the New Age music. I have found its use to be very beneficial. The concentration of the inner world is enhanced breaking new barriers. The harmony is magnified; the depth of the meditation full of wonder and delight. Wisdom has flowered on barren soil into a glorious bloom. My senses has multiplied a thousandfold.

The first cassette I listened to was Pathways to Love. I will describe the essence of beauty which is accentuated by music. I played the tape and I became excited and exhilarated in the meditation. I found it to be haunting. The melancholic chords put me in immediate touch with my beloved Zalmné. I did not use the cave to enter the inner world.

Zalmné was waiting for me by the pool. I said, "Can you hear the music?" He nodded, 'yes', and seemed pleased by it. "Let's listen together," I suggested.

We listened intently and it seemed have a positive effect on him. It lightened his mood which is always deeply solemn and reflective. He even become cheerful and laughed which is indeed a rare sight! The crescendo of it carried us into the hidden realms of the sublime.

We danced and danced twirling round and round on the pool. I was wearing a flimsy white chiffon dress edged with frills of gauze-lace. Zalmné was wearing his white tunic. He had two dove feathers in his headband.

Firstly, the Sun came to see what was going on. He joined us in our dance

41

of delight.

We danced on the water and we danced in the forest. The Sun following behind us dancing! We met the Fool. He liked the music and danced with the Sun. The High Priestess came out of her crystal cave, holding her baby.

I stretched out my arms saying, "Let me hold the baby." I took it from her and stepped in the sparkling lake. Several swans came forward and carried us to the middle.

I stepped lightly onto a giant yellow water-lily. The golden light of the Sun was warm and loving. The green light of the Fool was brilliant and enlightening and the psychic power of the High Priestess seeped inside me.

Under the combined influence of these powerful archetypes; I was aware of being on the higher plane. I sensed I was approaching the barrier of the mystical veil. I felt God's presence but did not see him fully. I could perceive a form in a long flowing white hooded robe; just visible beyond the flimsy transparent veil. It shrouded his face, still hidden from me but I know that it was God.

Then I heard a silent voice in my head.

No human however brave, can perceive past God's veil. When the time is right God's face will be revealed. When at last you see him your sorrow will disperse. Ultimate destinies to be accomplished. Death shall not hold you ever again.

I knew I was still on the higher plane. I was walking in the garden of Eden. I perceived the beginning of Adam (the life in heaven). The Eve (the destruction of the world), and the Snake (the death of the body). A simple pure beginning: A mighty struggle of human souls and then a penalty of heavenly judgement.

We returned to the inner world from our travel of the higher plane. I said farewell to my beloved guide and rejoined my earthly body.

Date of meditation: 2/7/91

MEETING THE SECOND GUIDE

My beloved was waiting for me by the pool; only this time he was not alone. Zalmné introduced me to my second guide; Suleman. I was not really sure of his origin. I thought perhaps he was Arabian or Indian.

Suleman wore a turban; which was of heavy grey brocade silk embossed with unusual designs and ancient patterns. In the middle of it; in a cluster of fine peacock feathers, was a large red-ruby mounted on a delicate gold-pin.

His pale grey light silk tunic fell straight to his thighs. Buttoned all the way down the front; it was tied loosely around the waist with a sash of deep-crimson. His loose pants of white silk ballooned at his ankles. On his feet he wore soft red leather shoes pointed and curling upwards. I noticed a white unicorn by his side. Zalmné said, "Suleman comes from the ancient kingdom of Solomon."

All of us stood together holding hands. I was in the middle. All of a sudden I felt a terrible sadness sweeping over me. I was very unhappy to be introduced to Suleman. I did not want to leave Zalmné. My heart filled with an internal pain. Tears streamed down my face. After I had sobbed and sobbed and was sufficiently recovered, Zalmné said, "We have to go."

He produced a long narrow canoe on the pool. I sat in the middle. Suleman sat behind me and Zalmné sat facing me.

The canoe, without being steered, took us out to sea. Eventually, in the distance I could see a misty shore. It was calm and the sun was low on the horizon. We reached the shore and stepped out on to a deserted beach. High in the rocks was a cave. Zalmné remarked. "This is where Suleman lives." Then I saw two beautiful unicorns romping on the golden sands. Zalmné said, "One of the unicorns shall be yours once you have been fully initiated by your second guide."

I surveyed the seascape. Below Suleman's cave, I saw rocks and pebbles strewn about. To the right of me facing the sea, the beach stretched as far as the eye could see. To the left of me the view was obscured by high cliffs and jutting rocks.

We mounted on his powerful black stallion and raced on the beach. The wind whipped my face blowing through my hair. I was exuberant and free as the wind and the sky. The rhythm and tranquillity lulled me back to a happy equilibrium and I was restful.

In a light manner I said, "Take me to see the Sun." Zalmné commanded his stallion to take flight. Instantly we were airborne and flew as before to the heart of the sun . Floating in its smoky-blue and yellow transparent spirit. It welcomed us. The rainbow-light shone in my inner-being. I felt the Sun's love surge in my inner-self, and my soul capitulated.

We descended back to Suleman's beach. Zalmné said, "I will leave you with Suleman, so you can get acquainted. I would like you to spend more time with him." I sat down miserably on a large boulder staring out to sea in total desolation; feeling morose and depressed.

"Don't wander too far!" I cried out, "I will miss you."
He promised he wouldn't.

I sat gazing at the misty horizon shrouded in a dusky twilight. Opulent colours slashed the sky. I sat like this for a long time in the-depths of misery and feeling lonely. Then I sensed that Suleman was standing behind me. Offering me comfort by his presence and reassuring everything would be all right by the slight touch of his right hand on my right shoulder, gently squeezing it in affection and warmth. All I said was, "Take me back to the pool."

He called his unicorn and we sat on it. It flew in the evening sky. We descended at the pool and Suleman left us.

I said in sadness, "I am not happy to be introduced to the second guide. Why is the transformation so soon?"

Zalmné replied, "I already know your heart, the introduction will be a gradual process. I will not leave you yet; you still have much to learn. Work with the guides as they appear before you."

He said, "Go and lie in the cool water., I will wash your sadness away." He came and bathed my ill-tempered brow soothing it.

I queried, "How am I to communicate with Suleman?"

He answered, "All communication in the inner world will be by thought-transference. There will be no verbal discourse. Mere words are insufficient to express the emotions. Your whole beings will commune."

I said farewell and reunited with my other body

Date of meditation: 3/7/91

THE REAL LOVE

I have now arrived at a point of realisation. I now know the name Zalmné means, 'The one who knows'. Since finding him I had been probing for answers about his existence in the inner world: I am convinced he is not an ordinary mortal; but one who is blessed with an extraordinary power of understanding beyond of the normal faculties of the human mind.

I approached him. All he said was, "You are going on a strange journey." Suddenly, I was flying having being transformed into a soaring white eagle. I flew high in the sky, traversing the dizzy heights of the heavens. Just as unexpectedly, I was no longer a white eagle but was transformed to a spirit! I was in a dimension I had never seen before and inspired to write these words.

> My spirit was drifting
> To a serene golden light,
> It pervaded my soul.
> I was uplifted to heaven
> And stood before God.
> Archangels Gabriel and Michael
> Carried me to the Temple of Love.
> The love soothed my heart
> Healing my great sorrow,
> I knelt before God and asked him,
> To heal the world,
> The pain and the darkness.

I asked for his love to permeate the universe, so that perfect harmony and beauty could be achieved. I asked for his love to transcend our hatred so that discord amongst humanity could be lessened. Lastly, I asked for his love for all people.

We descended back to the inner world from the upper dimension landing near Suleman's cave. I was very quiet. The strange journey had affected me. I was dizzy with elation. My head was still whizzing somewhere in the heavens, unable to return to the astral plane.

Suleman sensing this, grabbed my hand and pulled me onto his unicorn. He knew I liked flying on it, so he took me round and round the seascape to bring me back to the inner world.

We flew to the pool and then Suleman left. I told Zalmné that the unusual journey had affected me somewhat. He replied quietly, "Rest a while before you go back."

When my senses returned to normal, I said farewell and rejoined my body sitting deeply in meditation.

Date of meditation: 6/7/91

SPHERE OF HOD

LOOK WITHIN FOR GOD

Today I had difficulty in entering the cave and could not focus on the meditation. Eventually with hard concentration; I was beside the pool, and my beloved Zalmné was waiting for me.

His bow and arrow were casually slung over his shoulder in the long leather pouch. I thought he had been hunting. He was pleased to see me.

I had several questions on my mind to discuss. Zalmné nodded his head in response. He seems to have an uncanny knack of already knowing the root of my problems.

He summoned the High Priestess, Lady Moon and Lady Chariot to the gathering. They came: The awesome psychic power of the High Priestess touched me as she spoke, "When God awoke from His sleep he said, 'Who am I?' The earth was created and the God-Consciousness travelled in the plane of earthly life in human form. Then he placed in each man and woman his seed, so that his wisdom would be cherished for eternity."

The following was inspired by the High Priestess:-

Look not yonder for God,
For the is the One within.
He radiates inside your heart,
In each living thing.
His spirit flows everywhere,

45

His ethereal Love for the World.

The Revelation over, we sat sharing the pleasant interlude of companionship in a mutual bond of affection.

Date of meditation: 27/7/91

MANY LIVES AGO

I have been introduced recently to the New Age music. I played the tape, Many Lives Ago, whilst deeply meditating. I would recommend its beneficial use as an aid to meditation . It produces tremendous impact on the self; calming the inner-self. Immediately one is directly in touch with the sense evoking the explorative capacity to reach the hidden depths not normally available to the rudimentary five senses.

By listening to it; I achieved deep meditation almost instantly, drawn to the haunting mysterious melancholic sound. I was beside the pool. Zalmné wasn't alone; Suleman was with him.

Zalmné was standing up masterfully blowing the long humming sound of the huge horn. Suleman sat yoga-fashion drumming a tabla; making delicate movements with his soft palms.

Something strange stirred in my subconscious. I was ensnared by their music. I found myself dressed in flimsy white chiffon translucent robes with gossamer wings. I danced in swirling mists, enveloped in an azure ephemeral light.

Suddenly, unexpectedly, without any warning my guides transported me away from the delightful scene. We levitated in a cloudless white sky towards a distant Tor.

I stood inside the cool brick-temple and as I looked to the sun above I saw the spirits become as one. The sky-spirit descended to merge with the earth-spirit; gliding through me to the under-world. It encircled the whole sphere before returning to the source from whence it came.

Suleman mysteriously departed, and Zalmné and I sat astride his white stallion high up on Glastonbury Hill. I realised we were not alone. Someone was in our midst and I saw that it was King Arthur, sitting on a chestnut mare and attired in a suit of armour made of glistening silver. His mare's back was covered by a moonstone metallic cloth. He took us into a secret passage through a maze of underground tunnels. They branched out in all directions. At last we came to a Temple. It was constructed in silver; and was splendid in its silvery-iridescence. It was circular, open on all sides, with a dome, supported by solid silver pillars, on which were engraved heavenly figures.

In the middle of the magnificent temple was an ornamental chair resembling a throne, covered by a. silvery-cloth and embellished by myriad glittering jewels. I saw a lone figure sitting deep in contemplation. He seemed unaware of our presence. I did not need to ask who he was. I felt a warm rush of love which spread through my heart. In an instant I had the full knowledge. I felt the spirit move in one continuous motion; from the Upper Heaven (sky) to the Middle Heaven (earth) and the Under Heaven (underworld). One moving spirit enveloping our whole world.

The melodious music still played in the background, Zalmné and I returned to the inner world. I said farewell and rejoined with my physical body sitting upright in meditation.

Date of meditation: 29/7/91

SPHERE OF NETZACH

EDGE OF DREAMS

I was listening to the tape Edge of Dreams. Instantly I was transported to the pool. I approached Zalmné; he was standing near the water. For a short while we explored the depth of each other's love uniquely binding us in its invisible bond. suddenly, he stood up spreading his arms wide towards the sky, in deep contemplation.

I watched him in fascination. A mystical totem pole appeared in his right hand emerging out from the invisibility. A cobra slithered along its length moving over his still body, entwining around his arms and neck; crawling down his torso, legs and back. Then it moved upwards towards his third eye.

I was hypnotised by this unusual phenomenon and felt the power of the kundalini. Its explosive bliss resonating through every bit of my being, aware of his sacred knowledge, gradually being released into my psyche. The serpent just as quickly evaporated disappearing again in the invisible mists of time, only to come when called by the strange power of the inner guides.

Whilst my guide was still entranced in his meditation, I saw a white eagle fly in and perch on his right shoulder. It rested for a short while then flew to the middle of the pool, transforming magically into human female form. She danced before me her provocative dance an absolute perfection.

By this time all my inner senses were alert and alive, marvelling at the momentous moment and special significance of the inner world.

When my guide finished his meditation; I said farewell and reunited with my body.

Date of meditation: 8/8/91
7-30 PM approx. for half hour

THE BODILY PATH

I had been subconsciously aware for some time in meditation that perhaps the archetypes may be able to help and repair my worldly body. I have decided to ask Zalmné's advice on this matter; and for his assistance in achieving this. When I met him today at the pool, I asked if something can be done about my persistent back pain. Promptly he said, "You are suffering with the pain of the world. I will take you to the World archetype - Sir Lancelot, so you can understand healing and its associated aspects."

We flew on his white-winged stallion to the earth's axis where Sir Lancelot was waiting for us. He proceeded to use his strange power. An incandescent yellow laser beam and two hands appeared out of the black space. The laser beam cut open my back and the two hands retrieved the pain. Sir Lancelot said, "Go now and visit the Hermit. He will show you how to deal with your spiritual pain. I have dealt with the physical - but at the same time, your mental pain and sorrow has to be erased."

So we went to the Hermit. Sir Lancelot accompanied us. He told the Hermit my mental indisposition was causing the affliction and affecting the balance my reality.

The Hermit was sitting on his wooden box as usual. If I didn't already know him, I would feel sorry for him. But he is wise and has shown me his great wisdom. I admire his strong will and strength. He said, "Your sadness is related to the present time. There is much anguish around you. I will bring forth into your conscious the individuals responsible for your suffering." No sooner had he spoken then the ghostly forms of people trailed in one by one into my conscious mind. They rose from my subconscious mind, where they had been buried deeply. I hadn't realised how many people I had met had contributed to my pain.

The Hermit continued, "Now that you are consciously aware of the source of your grief, your life will be enriched; pathways will open and happiness much easier to grasp and handle. I would like you to visit the Chariot. She possesses deep insight into the power of healing. She will heal you bodily. I have healed you spiritually. She will also cleanse your 'chakras', so any negative Archetype cannot enter. You will be protected in all your domains. There are the sixteen vertical chakra points; the nine aural, and the seven hidden ones in the body which are the genitals, base of the spine, solar plexus, heart, larynx, forehead and the crown."

Zalmné and I returned to the pool and found the Chariot already waiting for us. She said, "I will take you to my healing chamber where I will relieve you of your penance."

The people in my mind went with us to witness. They stood around and watched as the Chariot worked: She took out each sorrow from my heart and gave it to the person responsible. Then she collected all them together, clasped them tightly and blessed them. She commanded that they be taken to the Fool, so he could bless all the hurt with his love, and thereafter to bury it deep under the earth to disintegrate and be forgotten.

The Chariot said,"I would like to give you more therapeutic sessions. Your mental pain has dispersed but the organic structure of natural disease can recur requiring, further treatment. If this is so, come and see me if you want my assistance in the future."

Zalmné raced his powerful stallion through the forest, and we were soon in the Fool's Land. We laughed and frolicked in the forest. We were not alone; the Star-Alien had joined us.

We went back to the pool and I lay in the limpid water to relax. Zalmné offered advice, "In addition to the healing you have received from the archetypes. I would like you to refrain from drinking any alcohol for three weeks. Instead, take plenty of water sweetened by honey and lemon. This will help rid the toxins. Abstaining from strong intoxicants, this will aid the meditation powers, the higher-self and chakras are affected by these stimulants. They are being choked, clogged; the inner-stimulus is unable to filter into the inner-self; clouding the judgement and perceived true reality."

After I regained my composure, I said farewell and once more re-entered my physical form.

Date of meditation: 10/8/91 9.00 AM

MEETING THE THIRD GUIDE

I was listening to the tape Atlantis. I found I was naturally in touch with the inner-world. Its crescendo carried me to the dizzy heights of delirium. Bliss was like a fever coursing through my soul.

Suleman emerged from the invisible mists of time accompanied by his unicorn. He sat astride the mystical creature as it hovered over the silken waters of the pool. His attitude was serene, and a radiance shone on his face as he looked upwards towards heaven as though in prayer. The magnificent ruby blazed, throwing a single beam of radiant red light which merged with the clear light descending downwards. I looked up to the sky and thanked God for showing me such wondrous beauty. Words cannot describe the vision.

We drifted from the pool flying over the green forest and the white sky. The melancholic chords carried me deep within myself as I flew over the desert, drifting over the desolate dunes. We descended, and in the far distance a moving silhouette came nearer. Then I saw a man sat on a camel.

He looked in his late thirties and as he came nearer, I noticed his deep-blue radiant eyes. I was mesmerised by them and stared as though I was hypnotised. He was dressed like a nomad, covered from top to toe. Only his bright eyes were showing. He seemed tall, attractive and appealing. We were silent waiting for him to speak but he only gestured. He beckoned for us to follow. We trailed behind him walked over the sandy dunes. On arriving at his camp we went inside his tent. An amber fire blazed and the shadows cast by the lamp made the place seem cosy, warm and welcoming. We stood around watching him, our eyes following his every movement.

He discarded his heavy over-garment revealing a full-length, cream, satin shirt, which was imprinted with fine vertical navy-blue stripes. He unwound his turban loosening his raven-black hair. It fell in .soft curls over his shoulders. Around his neck he wore a heavy gold chain and from it hung a large sapphire. Each facet gleamed and reflected the golden firelight. I said, "Who are you?" stressing my question. I was taken aback by his reply, "I am King Solomon, your third guide." I was truly amazed and a surge of astonishment and bewilderment passed straight through me.

I became quiet and slightly perplexed and pondered on meeting mighty Solomon. Zalmné read my thoughts and advised, "This introduction will be brief, you will meet Lord Solomon again."

We returned to the pool. Suleman strangely disappeared. This is his usual trick, he goes when we come back. We sat down on the grass beside the bank and talked. He said, "From now on before you go back to your physical world you must be cleansed by the Chariot."

We went to her healing cavern and she produced her white crystals as she closed all my chakras. At the same time she withdrew my pain, which she enclosed in her crystal dish and sent it across to the Fool, so that he could bury it.

I am overwhelmed by my guide's wisdom. He has shown me many of the mysteries of the inner world. I would like to remain here for always, but as he has said many times. "You must return to your earthly life. I exist for you within only to be your guide. My role is to teach you, and guide you on these treacherous plains. I will protect you and prevent you from becoming lost or being devoured by any negative archetype. You will retain the knowledge you acquire here, and become sublimely aware of the subtleties of the universe."

Date of meditation: 11/8/91 10.30 PM

SPHERE OF TIPARETH

THE INNER HEAVEN

I went to our usual meeting place, but Zalmné was not to be seen. I waited for him thinking he wouldn't be long as the fire had been lit. The amethyst-amber flames flared, fanned by the brisk-breeze. I thought the inner world is lonely without him. Occasionally, whilst I waited for him to appear, I became afraid, just as I sometimes am in my physical life. Just as I fear to walk alone in a field or fear being mugged, raped or brutally murdered. here I am frightened of things unseen, demons and devils devouring my very soul. I am terrified of being trapped in the deep-dimension. Frightened of the occult. Frightened that I will be unable to retrace my steps back from this bewildering maze.

It took a while for my guide to emerge out of his invisibility. By this time I was petrified looking this way and that. like an animal instinctively watching for danger. I saw him, just emerging from the dense forest. He wasn't alone. An Indian lady sat behind him astride his stallion, in the way I usually do. To my utter surprise and disbelief, Zalmné introduced us, "This is my wife," he said. I did not think a relationship was possible in the inner world? I did not know one could have a wife or husband. She dismounted and walked towards me. I thought, when will I learn and accept surprises?

After I recovered from my initial shock, I found myself warming to her. Instead of feeling pangs of jealousy I was filled with love. We embraced each other in joy and she pointing to her belly said, "I am with child." We sat around the fire and enjoyed the companionship. After filling my heart with contentment and friendship, Zalmné commented, "I will take my wife back to the camp."

I said, "Don't be too long, I am scared to wait alone." Zalmné communed silently with Suleman calling and summoning him to be by my side.

He arrived on his unicorn and brought the second one for me. We flew towards the beach and descended on the shore. I surveyed the seascape and absorbed its beauty, exclaiming suddenly, "It is so beautiful here, like heaven on earth."

Suleman was surprised and said, "It is heaven on earth." I asked him to explain and to take me inside his cavern.

He took me and I marvelled. The walls were lined with phosphorescent crystals. Its breath-taking incandescence dazzled me! I was enthralled by the enchanting scene and, delirious in inner joy.

I questioned him saying, "What did you mean, it is heaven on earth?"

He explained, "The inner world we stand in now is the astral plane. I come from the plane of Heaven. I have come to this dimension to be your guide. Through my guidance you will absorb the inner-knowledge which I will teach you."

He continued, "In the crystal cavern there are .seven secret doors, they have to be found. They are not openly visible to the seeing eye. 'These seven doors lead to the seven planes which inter-merge with each other. Like the seven secret doors; the seven planes are also invisible. If the seven planes were visible to the seeing eye we would not be shrouded in the mysteries of life. That is why the seven secret doors have to be hidden." I asked, "How does one find the seven secret doors opening to the seven planes?"

"Each door is guarded by a python; so huge it defies the imagination. When you find a door, which is the hardest task, you have to go past the massive snake. If you have the courage. On seeing that you have attained a high level of wisdom the snake will let you pass easily. It guards the passage with its venomous bite. If your knowledge is insufficient, entry is forbidden. The snake will threaten you by hissing. Without wisdom your search will be endless."

Without my asking him, he said, "The seven planes of knowledge are these: They are intermingled with the present now." He listed them as follows:

1.	The Death	The Unconscious
2.	The Birth	The Conscious
3.	The World	The Life
4.	The Astral	The Dream
5.	The Heaven	The Judgement
6.	The Mid-Heaven	God-Love
7.	The Upper-Heaven	God-Bliss

He continued to explain, "Besides these seven planes, there are six other higher planes. There are thirteen planes which a human soul has to pass through to attain the God-Consciousness. The higher planes are too complex for the ordinary human mind to comprehend. Before entering the higher planes the soul must acquire wisdom, through meditation and self analysis, and the help of the guides. Only when the soul has achieved absolute unity, can it comprehend the true-reality of the God-Bliss and share God's kingdom of eternal life."

He carried on, "On the six upper planes, the soul is united in the God-Bliss, after it has acquired the wisdom of the preceding seven planes. Once it has attained the knowledge of all thirteen planes it becomes like God; living in the eternal Spirit of the Divine. The union of man, woman and God is completed on the thirteenth plane. God alone exists as the Alpha and the Omega: The Creator and sustainer of all Life."

I must have been in deep meditation, for I felt the power of the kundalini in the pit of my belly. Waves of nausea erupting in my solar plexus. Coldness gripped me in its icy hands. I told Suleman I was feeling sick. In an instant he took me back to the reality of the inner world and to the welcome sight of his crystal cave. I rested for a. short while in its luminous translucence attempting to regain control of my senses which were still flying, somewhere on the higher planes.

Then I said, "Take me to the Chariot." We flew there on our unicorns. As we approached her crystal chamber I could see a misty shroud of pale lilac light. My guide waited for me whilst I was being healed.

I lay on the gilded couch in the middle of the cavern. The Chariot put her hands in my astral body withdrawing the internal pain - lifting it out. She placed it in a crystal utensil and sent it by her stallions to the Fool. He would bless it with his love before putting it to rest under the earth never to be found.

Suleman and I flew over the forest to my cave. Here, he said farewell and left me. I rejoined my physical body and opened my worldly eyes.

Date of meditation: 12/8/91 10.00 AM
Approximately one hour.

LAMENTATION

I was listening to the tape Atlantis, hypnotised by its haunting melody. It put me in touch with the inner world. As I neared the familiar pool, there was deep sorrow in my heart. I searched for Zalmné, but he was absent. Waves of sadness washed over me and tears welled in my heart, running down my cheeks.

I missed him terribly like one does after a lover's tiff. The absence seemed unbearable. I was full of remorse and memories. Vivid dreams engulfed me. I imagined we were still together, and whilst I was in the midst of recapturing the past in my fanciful imagination, Suleman must have arrived. Slowly I emerged from my dreams and became aware he was standing beside me. He was quiet in sympathy sharing my grief. He knew how I missed Zalmné. He took me on his unicorn flying around the seascape. He knew this calmed me. We descended back on the shore and I said, "I need to be alone to think." I went inside his crystal cavern and I prayed in solitude to ease my heavy heart. Then I walked up and down, like a thing possessed to be rid of my searing sorrow. The sea's serenity touched me, and I felt some momentary relief from a torment which was cutting me in two. Suleman sensing this, returned. I said, "I must go back."

Before I left the inner-sphere we went to the Chariot. Her cavern was aglow with a pale shimmering emerald light. She healed my wound with her transparent green crystals; withdrawing the hurt from my astral body and sent it to the Fool to be buried in the earth.

I said farewell to my guide and returned to my mortal world.

Meditation: 12/8/91   7.00 PM

VEIL OF THE GREATER MYSTERIES

LOVE AND BEAUTY

I went to the pool dejectedly knowing that Zalmné would not be at our usual meeting place.   I was surprised and bewildered when I   saw him standing serious and calm, staring deeply in the watery depths, but did not comment. I was happy to be with him.

He said, "Come, I will accompany you to meet Suleman, you must continue to learn." I did not fully understand what he meant. Nevertheless, we took the pathway leading to the beach. Zalmné didn't stay for long. We all meditated silently for a short while, then he left.

I was feeling really sad. I went to my unicorn and stroked it, feeling its inner beauty, appealing to my inner senses. Some joy returned tinged with sorrow. I sat astride its flank and it flew around the seascape healing the deep rift that Zalmné's absence had created. Slowly, I became happy, then dizzy with elation and exhilaration.

It descended near Suleman's cave. I stepped inside and found him kneeling in prayer. I joined him in his contemplation of the God. When we eventually finished I said, "I would like to meet Lord Solomon again."   Suleman summoned Lord Solomon using his mystical power of calling to send a message across the inner sky.

I waited in anticipation, then I perceived a golden chariot descending, drawn by four primrose-coloured stallions. It landed near us.

As soon as we were all together we immediately immersed in a deep, inner-search, especially me. I asked, "Where exactly am I at this moment in time?" They replied in unison, "You are in the astral world and we are your guides."

I questioned further, "What is the purpose of the inner-journey?" Again they   answered   together, "We are here to teach and you are here to learn. From our teachings you will awaken the self." Then King Solomon quietly confided, "I have come from the sixth plane." No further explanation was given. I asked him if it was true that one day the world would be destroyed. He did not directly answer me but simply said, "When one is not blind, the truth can be seen." I think I understood his meaning.

Then I asked him to convey a message to our Lord God from the bottom of my heart.

I beseech the Lord Almighty,

Who chooses to remain hidden from my mortal eye,

I pray to him,
Not to destroy our world,
To salvage the beauty
To save the population.

I ask Him from the seat of my heart,
Let my prayer not be wasted,
There is a new light dawning in the Aquarian sky,
Many hearts are full of love,
Many eyes have opened in the darkness.

Heal the world of depravity O Lord God.
I ask You O Lord Almighty,
Remember your promise made to Noah,
Not to annihilate the people.
Look and see the bright rainbow of Aquarius,
Arching over the new age.
Keep your covenant O Lord God;
Perish not any part of the earth,
The blue skies and green lands,
Kill not your love that rages,
In the hearts of men.
Let your clear light shine,
Carried on the wings of your mighty angels.

Heal the world of its pain O Lord God.
Let the passion within awaken,
By the inner man and woman.
The love and beauty to be taken,
To keep infinitely within.
Treasure it like a sacred-medicine,
Take it to ease the inner-pain.
Within our subconscious we have in vain,
Attempted to rid this sorrow which persists within.
Take a stroll in the planes of the Divine,
Catch the love and beauty of that plane.
This sacramental ethereal beauty truly sublime,
Disperses tides of tears from within.
Let the Godly passion awaken,
To be taken by each man and woman.
Lord Solomon ascended up towards to the sixth heaven. Suleman came

with me to the Autumn pool.   I was delighted to see beloved Zalmné once again. I was happy to be with him.. We contemplated for a short while.

I said, "Take me to the Chariot."

This time her cave was suffused in luminous green light. I lay on the green-covered couch and she produced her green crystals and passed them over my body, and then with her delicate hands she drew out the pain in my womb. She then sealed all the chakras and sent it to the Fool to be buried deep under the earth.

Zalmné, accompanied me to the cave. On the way we strolled on the bank of the High Priestess' lake. She appeared again as Lady Mary with the baby in her arms. Her companions were the white swans. She smiled at me serenely and I smiled back returning her pleasant gesture. I looked at her; I saw her wisdom shone radiant in her eyes touching the depth of my soul.

As we neared the entrance to my exterior-world, I gently squeezed Zalmné's arm in affection before letting him return into the inner world.

Date of meditation: 16/8/91

ENLIGHTENMENT

I went via the cave into the inner world to the familiar pool, but alas beloved Zalmné was not waiting.   I was deeply tormented and saddened by his absence. It took me a while to gather my inner-strength. I was at a loss to understand his reasoning; leaving me so shortly and quickly.   After a profound inner-search, I carried on walking towards the beach.

I stood on the sandy shore feeling the breeze and listening to the rhythmic euphonic sea. In the far distance I saw Suleman. Then he came over to join me.

We contemplated for a while as it has become customary to meditate in the inner world. My love for him is slowly beginning to blossom in my heart. It is a gentle kind of love, soft and tender. Not the pressing fabulous type I feel for Zalmné.

After our inner-meditation I asked him many questions pertaining to the soul and its journey through life, and the supposedly different identities it takes through reincarnation. I asked him if reincarnation was true.

He gave me an answer, but I was unable to understand the breadth of his wisdom. I realised I have not yet arrived at the secret door. I have not acquired sufficient knowledge to pass behind the invisible wall.

Then I asked him about the Holy Books of Religion. The Torah, Bible, Quran and Bhagavad-Gita, asking him what they actually symbolise and whether they contained the truth.

Suleman replied, "In the beginning God was the only knowledge. Then He formed the earth, and in it, man, beast, bird and serpent. Throughout time

56

there have been countless theories on his existence. Behind all the facade the one truth remains, the godly force that sustains our life."

He continued to expound on life and death, and the dawn of a bright sun daily unceasingly, automatically. The rise of the shining moon in our dark sky. The wonders which manifest from God. He said, "As to your question on the books of religion; they serve to teach mankind so that his ever-expanding consciousness can grasp workings of God. Without knowing how Life came into being man would exist like the shadows, dimly aware, not fully conscious, that he has the inner-power to catch the eternal wisdom swirling around him."

He continued his discourse, "Man is on the way to becoming, By this I mean everything is in a state of becoming. It moves transiently in the threads of life; weaving this and that. Then once the fabric has been woven, it remains for a while in a fixed state. After sampling the fixed state, the fabric unthreads and moves once more onto becoming. The man, soul and spirit are like the fabric which evolves; the fabric materialises and dematerialises, countless times in aeons in becoming and fixed states. The process goes on indefinitely; the energy is not wasted. It flows continuously in the surges of life and death, gathering momentous knowledge in the wake of its movements on the highest plane of living. The human is living life combined of the elements of the soul and earth matter. The body and spirit are the realities assumed by the Soul. We are on our way to integrating with the one whole. The existence of the Body, Soul and Spirit are vital in our journey of becoming conscious."

Suleman and I flew back on. his heavenly unicorn to meet Zalmné. He was sitting on his stallion. He held his hand out for me. I clasped it and he pulled me up. I held on tightly around his waist as he galloped in the forest. As we were riding I mentioned the pain in my back was still hurting.

He said, "It is the pain of the physical. You must continue with the healing from the Chariot. She will help you. Now I will take you to your cave." We said farewell and I returned to my body.

Time of meditation: 8.00 AM - 17/8/91

THE JOURNEY OF THE SOUL

I went to meet beloved Zalmné at the pool but he was absent. I thought I will go and see Suleman. I followed the dove onto the path leading to the beach.

I looked for Suleman in the crystal cave, but it was empty. I called, "Suleman, Suleman, where are you?" without any response.

I walked on the golden sands and stood staring at the sparkling sea. I saw someone swimming in the far distance, and thought, that must be Suleman. At last he saw me. When he stepped out of the water, I couldn't help grinning.

I made a concentrated effort in keeping the mirth to myself, otherwise I would have laughed aloud at the ridiculous way he looked; very comical indeed. He was nearly naked, apart from a white muslin cloth tied loosely around his genitals. He might not have bothered to wear anything ! I could see straight through the transparent wet material! Another thing was his large protruding belly. I hadn't realised, he was rather plump. He walked past me, sensing he looked foolish.

When he came out dressed, I thought, he looked quite nice. He wore a light grey silk tunic and loose balloon pants in a lighter silk of the same colour.

I questioned him on reincarnation. His reply astounded me.

"In reality, nothing really exists." I asked him to elucidate.

He explained, "Each incarnation is not another body with an individual soul, but the one enlightened soul assumes various bodily guises to perfect itself on the thirteen planes. In its rudimentary state, it is conscious of only one plane at a time. But when it has mastered all the planes of wisdom, it is conscious of all realities at one given moment. God is the reality of all the planes for all eternal time. The human soul is comprised thus and traverses the realities of life and death on the structure of the inner wisdom. The soul, spirit and body survive on the thirteen planes of wisdom:

      1. The Under-Heaven.

      2. The Life.

      3. The Death

These three are the body-realities

      4. The Astral

      5. The Heaven

      6. The Upper Heaven

These three are the spirit-realities.

The Seventh Plane Is Total God Unity.

8th 9th and 10th Planes The Enlightened (Submerged in God-Love).

11th 12th and 13th Planes,

The Intoxicated Planes: (Eternally conscious of God-Bliss)

"God is the Alpha and the Omega, The first and last, the Immaculate and Supreme Being."

Suleman carried on explaining, "The Karmic law takes effect on the first six planes. The human's actions of good and bad imprint reality on the structure of the soul. It is almost similar to Snakes and Ladders. The human's bad deeds take him to the lower levels of Karmic law and his good deeds place him at the top. In the strictest sense the one soul assumes different guises. Like in a theatre one wears different costumes, and as the act evolves one is aware of the plot. The one soul then manifests on all levels of realities having acted in the theatres of life and death. When at last it rests on the highest plane, having unravelled the mysteries of life, then, the knowledgeable soul will recognise its last guise on the stage of life; and the awakened reality of the perfected body and soul will integrate in the vast consciousness of God."

He continued, "The last God-Plane is the highest; in which He dwells in every aeon and eternity. He reigns supreme in the highest form of reality; and makes us conscious of our awareness of Him: He creates the same destiny for us, to follow his path to achieve the same eternal bliss He lives in forever."

When I came out of this inner-contemplation, I did not waste any time in returning to my physical body. I said, "I must go back quickly, before the ego and the unconscious, devour all the information I have received of the higher planes."

I made a hasty retreat and returned to write the wisdom I had been given by my guide.

Date of meditation: 22/8/91
2.30 PM

THE BEAUTY OF THE ANIMAL

I was once more beside the Spring pool of the inner world. This time Zalmné came to me; like the first time I saw him. I put my arms around his waist and hugged him in joy.

We sat down on the cool luxuriant grass without speaking. He stretched out and relaxed. I've never seen him like this before. I sensed something odd was about to happen. All my inner senses opened like a flower to the warmth of the sun; the fragrance drifting on the light summer breeze.

Our sweet telepathic discourse began by me saying. "I would like to see more animals. Apart from seeing the snake, dove, stallion and unicorn, I have not seen many." Then as I was communicating I glanced in the water. To my amazement, Zalmné was sitting into a yoga position contemplating in the watery depths-fully clothed.

I could see him clearly as the pool was crystal-clear, and inviting. I joined him and we shared together the quiet contemplative repose.

After a fair while, I opened my eyes. At first the images were blurred weaving this way and that, just like a mirage. And as I looked, the animals came to drink one by one. First to arrive were the mystical unicorns absolutely divine in the filtering light. Next on the scene were the black stallion and the white stallion, splendid and fabulous. Then at edge I saw white deer graceful and nervous. Next came a sleek panther, proud and arrogant. I was surprised he did not attack the deer.

The noise of their drinking reached my inner ear as my higher senses opened allowing me to become at one with all the wondrous beauty of the animals, the forest and the trees. I was attuned to my environment. I became at one with all and my fear subsided.

In all the glory surrounding me; I became aware of the power my guide exerted over the elements around him. He was totally in touch with his higher-self. Through his secret teaching, I have similarly come to know myself.

I sensed his pure love and the divine wisdom he was capable of. After experiencing our blissful states; we returned to the Autumn pool.

I crossed over to the other side and I was instantly united in the ephemeral love of the Star-Man and Moon-goddess. We laughed and frolicked in the green-lit forest.

Afterwards, I retraced my steps to my guide. He always waits patiently for me whilst I am united in the psychic union. I asked him to take me to the Chariot. We went to her cavern and a bright pink glow radiated outwards from within. I lay down on the pink covered couch. With the pink crystals, she practised her mystifying healing. She moved them over my body remarking at the same time, "This will stop the negative energies from entering."

Zalmné accompanied me to the cave. We said farewell at the entrance. I waved and stepped in to return to my exterior world.

Date of meditation: 27/8/91

THE ALIEN ENCOUNTER

I went to our usual meeting place but Zalmné was absent. So I followed the familiar path leading to the beach. Suleman was standing absolutely still on the tranquil seashore gazing out to the sea in deep meditation. I went over and stood beside him adopting the same manner joining him in the inner-search.

When we finished the contemplation he said, "Come, we will go on a flight." I sat on my unicorn and he on his. We soared in the sky. The immense blackness whizzed by past the glitter and sparkle of the stars. Finally, we arrived at our destination, the Moon.

The Moon-goddess was waiting for us. From the surface we travelled to the core to her massive glistening lake. The transparency touched by a deep blue luminescence. Translucent crystal forms of various colours hung from the cavern's ceiling. Particles of pink frost-ice floated in mid air and a silvery phosphorescent drifted over the expanse. The enigmatic enchantment, almost pure, untouchable and intangible.

I stripped and stepped in the sparkling lake; exalted by its lovely essence. The Moon-goddess and the Star-Man joined me in my intense pleasure. Then I was dimly aware, other aliens were swimming around us.

One of the aliens, I remember most vividly. He was small; four feet tall; snake-like in appearance with scaly skin. Green in colour with a tiny face resembling an ant.

He offered to show me his planet. We stepped in his mushroom shaped ship and zoomed past the myriad galaxies. There were no windows in it, but I watched the stars rushing by on the huge cinematic screen.

Eventually we arrived at his planet. It was covered in thick ice. As the ship descended to the inner-core, the alien sprayed a sealing chemical to protect me, explaining, "This will stop you from freezing over."

It seemed we were in a busy space-port. There were a dozen spaceships ascending and descending ferrying passengers.

We went down in a lift. Finally, we stepped into a room full of bright blazing lights. The room was constructed in a shiny metal, and robots were busily engaged in directing the space-traffic.

We stepped inside a transparent bubble. It floated in the air into the city. Their homes were like boxes, made from the same shiny metal. The light being artificial; a pale effervescent green for daytime and a heavier darker green for night use. Zen said, "We do not need to sleep like humans."

I thanked the Volien for showing me around his planet Vol. Then we zoomed back to the Moon. We said farewell and promised we would meet again.

Suleman and I flew in the silvery starry night and descended at the Autumn pool. Zalmné was waiting for me. I went straight to his stallion and nuzzled it in affection. He remarked, "You have seen the alien?" I nodded, "Yes."

We went to visit the Chariot and I said, "I have forgotten to ask for a gift." She produced a scintillating ruby that flashed with crimson-fire. She said, "I am putting this on your lower spine. It has a dual purpose. Firstly, the psychic energy will become more vibrant. Secondly, your spiritual vision will collate more insight. The kundalini will be alive and moving within you."

She sealed all my chakras, explaining that negative vibrations would not be allowed to enter. Shortly, I left the inner world. Walking in the forest with my beloved guide, leaving him in the clearing, I entered the cave and then my body.

Date of meditation: 28/8/91 7.30 am

THE DEATH FORM

Today it was very difficult to contact the inner world. The meditation mind was not focusing properly. With a mighty internal struggle to shift the ego's ambivalence presence, I eradicated its ambiguity, with an intense concentration, drifting slowly into the inner world.

Beloved Zalmné was not at the Autumn pool. So I followed the dove to the beach.

I was standing on the sands at the edge of the forest. I stood for a minute surveying the scene that lay before me. The atmosphere did not feel right. It was heavy and dull like that preceding a storm. Everything was deathly silent.. It is that precise moment when one is aware of an unknown presence, yet the mind is unable to fathom it!

I called Suleman. To my surprise he and Zalmné appeared from the misty inner sphere. They acknowledged me but remained silent. I broke the silence speaking first, "The ego and the swirling mind-thoughts keep dragging me back to my exterior realities. It is very hard today to remain in the meditation. What shall I do?" I moaned in despair.

Zalmné said, "Go and stand near the sea. Open your arms wide out towards the sky. Feel the psychic energy in you. Let the wind whip the green dress around your body. Combine your inner senses to the rhythm of the waves and feel the power of the gifts pulsating within your self."

I did as he asked. Instantly unusual sensations empowered me. Sacred knowledge transmitting deep into the centre of myself; the solar plexus. I was exhilarated beyond belief affiliated in harmony.

A huge goddess hovered over me imprinting upon the inner sky. She was quite large and not particularly beautiful but possessing much psychic prowess which she successfully transferred into me. We became as one in a powerful unity.

After the fulfilment of the goddess' love I became aware of a cobra slithering near me. It crawled all over my body moving further up the torso near to the crown. I felt its movements across my body descending to the solar plexus and then the genitals. I had been intensely aware of its movements. Highly sensitive, frightened and enlightened at the same time. I felt its mystical power had touched the depth of my soul.

In the intensity of the deep-level meditation I became the snake on the sand. I saw death before me in the form of a sandman with an axe, ready to strike and chop off my head. I unleashed my venom with fear lashing at the air. My scaly length thudded on the ground. In trepidation I sensed: death was near, but at the precise moment of dying; similar to that of a terrible nightmare, when one awakens suddenly, I was released from this ghastly torment. Thankfully my guides had stopped further interaction with the snake and the sandman.

I asked, "What was the reason for all that?"

The Sun	The Solar/central	Masculine	Spiritual
The Moon	High Priestess	Feminine	Psychical & Mother
Uranus	Fool	Masculine	Light
Mercury	Magician	Masculine	Illusion
Pisces	Moon	Feminine	Dream
Venus	Empress	Feminine	Love
Aries	Emperor	Masculine	Father
Taurus	High Priest	Masculine	Mystical
Gemini	Twins	Masculine & Feminine	Double Love (God`s and Human)
Cancer	Chariot	Feminine	Passion
Leo	Strength	Masculine	Faith
Virgo	Hermit	Masculine	Loneliness
Jupiter	Wheel of Fortune	Masculine	Money
Libra	Justice	Masculine	Judge
Neptune	Hanged Man	Masculine	Abyss
Scorpio	Death	Masculine	Dying
Sagittarius	Temperance	Masculine	Time
Capricorn	Old Pan/Devil	Masculine	Lust
Mars	Tower	Masculine	Holy Grail
Aquarius	Star	Masculine	Alien
Pluto	Last Judgement	Masculine	Revelation
Saturn	The World	Masculine	Life

They explained,"This has been a lesson to learn about death."

"I am still very frightened." I gasped in fear. Suleman kindly replied, "Go and lie in the sea and feel the cooling breezes on your face. You will become calm."

Zalmné and I left shortly after to go and visit the Chariot. As we neared her cavern, there was as an ice bath filled with blue crystals, which she placed all around my body. It was delightfully cool, and the coolness refreshed me, and soon tranquillity returned. She sealed my chakras with a touch of her delicate hands, so that the inner-wisdom would be contained within; and any negative invasions of the archetypal forces kept out of the self.

Zalmné walked with me to the entrance of my exterior world, and I held his hands tightly before I let him go. My love is intense for him. I cannot describe why or how. It has been one of those impossible dreams which has come true. He instils in me so much happiness. I came back to my worldly body reluctantly. I really did not want to. I wanted to remain with him forever, but he does not let me stay. He returned me unscathed to my physical body.

Date of meditation: 1/9/91 9.00 AM.

THE SACRED LOVE

Once more I had difficulty in entering the inner world. With much deliberation and concentration I succeeded in conquering the ego's persistence and the mind's fanciful swirling thoughts. Gradually, iridescent hues of the astral sphere filtered in, replacing the darkness in the meditation.

Eventually, Zalmné came into being waiting for me by the transparent sparkling water. I felt a little deflated and flat. I stared blankly ahead without speaking. We meditated for a while; then in the deep-level meditation, the meaningful realisations of all the archetypes were revealed.

Afterwards, I asked a very straight forward question. "What is love?" He did not reply, instead by his unknown power, I suddenly realised we were standing on the bank of the High Priestess' lake. She was transformed to the lovely vision of Lady Mary holding the innocent child in her arms.

I proceeded to ask her, "What is love?" repeating the question for the second time. She stepped forward out of her misty shadows surrounded in a pearly white glimmering light. As she came nearer her radiance became even brighter. In the clearness a vision focused wavering as in a mirage. The child had disappeared from Lady Mary's arms and had become the man standing before me. The Lady Mary said, "What you perceive now is real love." Her wise words touched my heart. I fell on my knees in wonder and. joy. The man laid his right hand on my head. I was totally drowned in his divine love. He said, "Take this, my flame of love in your right palm from my right palm." He produced a single flame burning in his right hand, similar to a candle flame. I took it from him giving him all my love in return.

Then Lady Mary spoke, "Take this, my flame of love in your left palm from my left palm." As before; I took it from her. She remarked gently, "By taking the flames from us, you will be made complete."

After the flames burned in both my palms, it radiated even brighter in my psyche. Its massive psychic energy transmitting to my inner-self, symbolising the love of heaven and the unity of God, man and woman. The phantoms then vanished, making the union of spiritual love more complete.

I said to my guide, "Take me to the Chariot." When we got near the cavern, a brilliant white light glowed from within. Its brilliance hurt my eyes, and the myriad of dazzling rays illuminated the deep mystery.

I sat down on the white silk-covered couch. The love suddenly erupted between us. For the first time the Fool came to join us. We shared the comradeship together. The spiritual love made more complete by the interaction of the great archetypes combined in total harmony, affinity and purity.

Zalmné and I rode together on his mighty stallion through the forest. At the entrance to the cave we said farewell. I held his hand tightly, and the pebble's power bonded our love perfectly.

I stepped inside the cool dim cave and into my own body.

Date of meditation: 2/9/91 - 8.00 AM

THE SILENCE

The swirling mists of darkness in the deep meditating-mind gave way to the dim shadowy light of the inner-cave: Then I stepped into the familiar landscape of the astral-world.

I followed the spiritual dove to my guide, but Zalmné was not at the Spring pool. I stepped inside the short secret tunnel leading to the Autumn pool but I did not find him.

I carried on to the beach and walked on the irregular path through the trees. On arriving there I called, "Suleman, Suleman. Where are you?" Without any response.

I studied the seascape. It was effulgent in enthralling hues; quite fabulous and fantastic. The two mystical unicorns, their beauty magnifying the splendid scene. A soft white mist swirled over the translucent waves. The silver-edged fluffy clouds moved in the unseen wind. The green frothy tides lashed on the golden sands. The beach receded in the distance to the hazy horizon and vanished from my vision. I thought: If I am not in Paradise now, then, I have no idea where I could be.

Two silhouettes on horse-back were etched against the misty sky. As they came nearer, I realised it was Suleman. I thought the other person was Solomon, but to my surprise it was a woman.

I noticed she was wearing heavy garments, covered from top to bottom similar to a nun's habit, but made of a sandstone-coloured material. It looked like tweed. I thought it was very unusual, and wondered why she was wearing such heavy clothing in the hot blazing sun. I could not see her face properly, it was obscured. She was a stout women, big-boned, plump and tall. Her manner seemed serene and tranquil.

I was most surprised when they didn't stop and greet me. In fact they seemed oblivious to my presence. I stared at them in astonishment as they passed by not even looking at me. I watched them dismount at Suleman's cave and go inside.

I was a bit deflated and put out that they had not addressed me. I became dispirited and miserable as I took the path to the Autumn pool. This time I was more fortunate, I found beloved Zalmné waiting for me in the usual place, but uncannily he remained silent.

I couldn't understand it. Everything was silent. Without speaking we contemplated then strolled to the Chariot's cavern. There was a pastel pink glow shining in her chamber. She appeared to be resting, but didn't seem irate at being disturbed. In fact her greeting was warm and friendly, although she did not say a word. She performed her healing in complete silence. Then she bathed me in tepid water filled with pink crystals before dusting me with the talcum of sandalwood. Slowly she removed the pain from my body and sent it to the Fool to be buried under the earth.

Zalmné and I walked hand in hand towards the cave. Whilst saying farewell, I thought, this has been an uncanny trip, not a word was said by anyone.

I returned to my body.

Date of meditation: 3/9/90 - 7.00 AM

SPHERE OF YESOD
FURTHER HEALING

I went straight to Zalmné's beach, bypassing the pool. Immediately on contacting him, I said, "Take me to the archetype who can heal my

monthly pain."
He transported us with his unseen power to the palace of the Empress. Her greeting was warm and friendly. I asked her to heal me. She proceeded by cutting open my back, working on the internal organs using her bare hands. She withdrew the pain and I could see it. It came out like a long piece of negative film, and as she pulled, more and more came out.

I thought it was most odd that I could see my pain this way. The Sun then gave it love and warmth to hasten the curing process. The Chariot touched it with her purifying crystals. The pain was enclosed in a crystal utensil and sent to the Fool to be buried in the earth.

I had witnessed the whole process with fascination. Suleman advised me to be conscious of the inner-healing. To be positively aware of it and to relish the assistance of the archetypes.

I said farewell to Suleman and entered my physical body.

Date of meditation: 4/9/91 - 3.00 PM

LIFE AND DEATH

I followed the spiritual dove to the pool. Zalmné was waiting for me.

I said, "Take me to see Death, I have forgotten to ask for a gift."

We searched for Death, but instead found Temperance. He was walking across a lonely field. I stopped him and asked. "Where is Death?" He replied, pointing to the far distance. "You will find him over there." I asked Temperance to call him to join us.

Temperance called silently across the inner-sphere. Death suddenly arrived galloping fast on his powerful black stallion. He was clad totally in black from top to toe. Only his glowering eyes showing through the narrow slits. The silky-black material draped across his form and over the stallion. Death spoke outright, "You have been avoiding me?"

"Yes," I replied, "I have been shunning you as I didn't really want to meet you. I am afraid of you. I don't understand you."

He replied casually, almost nonchalantly, "It is my job to take life. I have been appointed to do the work. I can't say I enjoy it. It is a necessary function which has to be undertaken by someone."

Candidly, I enquired, "Can you tell me what to expect after death."

He answered, "Because of the cosmic law which governs life, I am forbidden to answer your question. You are not allowed to know the secret of life and death. But know this, I will encloak you only temporarily."

Then I said, "May I have your gift? I did not ask for it when last we met." He produced a black onyx stone about one and half inches in length. "Put this in the cavity of your vagina. When you have assimilated its wisdom; you will attain a much wider understanding of my existence."

67

He carried on speaking, saying, "I will lift my dark veil. for a brief moment for you to see the other side." In the vision that I saw, my earthly father was standing by a stream in a beautiful garden. Other people were with him enjoying the peace and tranquillity. He seemed content and happy. I was pleased to see him this way. The vision dispersed and the dark veil was lowered once more.

Death and Temperance came with Zalmné and me, to search for the Hanged Man. When I saw the Hanged Man hanging from a tree I said, "Death, give him back life, so I can speak with him." Death obliged willingly and cast his power. Instantly the dead man stirred into life.

I had forgotten to ask for his gift the last time we met, so I said, "Please give me your gift and tell me its meaning."

The Hanged Man replied, "The only material thing I possess in this life is the rope I am hanging from. I will give you a piece of it to wear on your right ankle. Every time you look at it; you will remember my plight. This way you will be more aware of the error within you. When you see me next; stand before me and touch your right palm to my left foot and your left palm to my right foot. Then I will come alive to talk to you."

Then Death and Temperance returned to their abodes. We returned to the pool to contemplate. Shortly, we went to visit the Chariot. Today, her cavern was lit by a radiant lilac glow.

We called the Empress to come. Thereafter, the healing was undertaken by the ladies. The pain in both lower tibia-bones was physically taken out by the Empress and blessed by her love. The Chariot cherishingly enclosed it in a crystal utensil and sent it to the fool to be buried deep in the earth. Zalmné and I rode to my cave. This time he actually stepped inside to say farewell. I held his hand briefly and moved away from him rejoining my body.

Date of meditation: 5/9/91

THE OLD PAN

I searched in the darkness of my mind focusing on the mental triangle; upon the colours, and found the cave. I moved forward to the entrance facing me and stared at the scene below. There were several other caves dotted around the mountainside. The green grass sparse and patchy, grew in clumps. Irregular gravel paths lead down to the serene beach. The sky cloudless like a sheet of blue-ice. The sea sparkling bright like an emerald. The sand the colour of bleached calico. The seagulls screech and hover, hunting for fish.

I retreated back into the cave and touched the wall on my left, and found myself transposed into the inner-landscape. I was standing on a straight

68

gravel path which receded and disappeared from my view. To the left of me lay a small clearing, in front of the huge forest. To the right of me, my vision was obscured by tall trees and thorny shrubs. I turned to face the clearing, noticing the different saplings sprouting here and there. Faintly, I heard murmuring running water. I listened intently, my senses becoming alive.

My inner voice commanded the spiritual animal. The dove came. I said, "Take me to my guide."

It flitted from tree to tree, waiting for me if I lost sight of it. When my guide appeared in my visual field, the dove mysteriously disappeared.

I found Zalmné at the Autumn pool. I told him straightaway. "I feel very sad. On TV last night, was a programme about the how last of the Yahi were wiped out; and how the last one died. How can man inflict such cruelty to fellow-man? I would like to offer prayers of lamentation."

He contacted the dead with his eloquent chanting, then said. "They have been blessed by your remembering them. They are happy they will not be forgotten but are remembered in your prayer."

I said, "Take me to the Old Pan. I have forgotten to ask him for his gift." Zalmné and I transported instantly to the Land of Evil. There were half-eaten humans writhing and moaning in agony hanging from the trees. Their terror and torment was unbearable to see. The acute horror was pitiful. I felt repulsed and sick in the stomach. Several naked women sprawled on the ground with their legs wide apart, displaying their swollen genitals and mouths, enflamed by the lust of Pan.

The light was dim and the atmosphere dank. Thick fog swirled around the ghostly trees. Terrifying screams could be heard. The three demon witches guarded the Devil's cavern; absorbed in their ominous incantations, brewing dreadful potions. They cackled with evil laughter, like crows as we passed them to go inside.

The Old Pan was fast asleep; long drawn out whistling snores escaped from his open detestable mouth. Saliva mixed with fresh blood oozed down his abhorrent chin. Contempt and hatred for him surged in my heart.

He stirred and opened his slitty red eyes; the green pupils blazed with greed. Yellow pus encrusted in the their corners and dribbled down his cheeks.

I could not help but notice his phallus, it was red-raw and big. As soon as he set eyes on me he proceeded to masturbate, at the same time inviting, "Come and join me." I must admit to having been aroused by his temptation. The pulsating lust throbbed in my womb. I managed to resist his offer with a conscious controlled determination. I looked at my guide to see his reaction. He nodded his head brusquely from side to side as if to signify "no."

I stood over the Old Pan in fear and nervously asked, "Can you give me your gift and tell me its purpose?" I was startled when he spoke, "I am giving you a silver chalice to hold in your left hand. It is filled with sweet and bitter wine. I have tasted both, but as I am the bearer of darkness, I have to drink the bitter wine forever. I have been appointed to lead men into hell.

I am the bitter wine which flows in their hearts. If they had taken the sweet wine, their hearts would be like soft sugar candy. Savour both wines to aid you on your spiritual progress, but remember, the sweet wine will be your salvation on the path."

I must admit, I was surprised by the Old Pan's gift and his speech, but nevertheless, his appearance was scathing and I wanted to leave quickly.

I found it impossible to breathe in this dark putrid evil-smelling place, with its overpowering stench of stale sex, rotting bodies and corruption.

We instantaneously transported out of this terrible cavern. Whilst in transition, I said, "Take me to the Empress, I want to feel her love, to be rid of the wickedness I have just seen."

She greeted us warmly, at the same time commenting, "I have prepared for you a camphor bath. This will refresh and ease you after your encounter with the devil."

I lay in it and relaxed, only stepping out after a long leisurely soak. She dried me with soft fluffy warm towels and massaged me with the warmed oil of camphor, concentrating on my lower tibia bones to ease the pain.

The Empress then literally lifted the pain away from the bones and handed it to the Sun, who blessed it with his profuse warm love. Then it was sent to the Chariot in the crystal dish. She gave it further treatment with her special coloured crystals. It was finally given to the stallions to take to the Fool, who would bury it deep under the earth, never to be retrieved.

We rode on Zalmné's stallion to my cave. Just before entering, I turned and waved, noticing that his father was beside him. I stepped into the dim shadowy light, uniting once more with my body.

Date of meditation: 6/9/91 8.00 - 8.30 AM

THE ARCHETYPAL LOVE

I let my mind move into the meditation stopping the flow of annoying mind-filling thoughts, by adopting the procedure of the 'movement of the mind', concentrating on the electrifying colours of the mental triangle which helps me to submerge deeper into the meditation. Today, I was fortunate. The inner world focused easily, and I was standing next to the Magician, on the bank of his boiling bubbling lake.

I called for a guide. Suleman arrived, followed by the Star and the Sun.

As such mighty archetypes were assembled on the bank of the lake, I took the opportunity of asking for their help; to heal those parts of me which needed a lot of understanding.

The Star-Alien massaged me with a clear white star-liquid; the Magician washed me with his pure water and the Sun healed me with his penetrating warmth.

After the healing, I requested, "Take me to my Shadow." When we finally found her I couldn't see her properly. She was ghost-like and transparent. Then I heard a voice in my head say, "Go and look for her in the forest."

We went to the woodland of Uranus where the Fool lived. I saw my Shadow distinctly and clearly standing quietly and serenely under a tree. She was accompanied by her mystical stag. It adopted the same posture as its mistress - observant and statuesque as though, waiting for something to happen.

Instantly I was attracted to her calm beauty. She looked about twenty-five years of age and approximately five and half feet in height. Her luxuriant black hair resting on her shoulders in wavy curls. She was totally naked; quite well proportioned and curvy. Her pale skin glistened in the green-lit forest.

I noticed her looks weren't particularly outstanding but she possessed an air of carefree abandonment. She seemed to suffuse with her environment, as if merging with every creature in the forest, every plant and every tree.

For some obscure reason, we did not speak. I was glad of the silence, I didn't feel. like speaking. I was amazed and speechless. I stared at her in fascination.

Suleman interrupted and I heard his voice saying, "Come, that is enough for now. You will meet her again."

I said, "Take me to the Wheel of Fortune." When it eventually came into view, it was in the same form as last time. I asked, "Can you become a humanoid?" It did not respond and I was agitated so I ignored it and instead said to my guide, "Can you bring the World-Humanoid?"

He sent his silent call across the inner-sphere. The World came, transforming to a humanoid. He was as a man wearing a black suit and white shirt, carrying a black leather briefcase.

For the second time I said to the Wheel, "Can you change?" This time it obliged. He transformed into a weary bank official dressed in a black business suit and white shirt, carrying a black briefcase.

They stood before me and confessed: "We are weary from the toil of our professions." The Wheel continued, "I am tired of handling the affairs of men." The World said, "I too am tired of sorting the affairs of men."

They did look pale and worn-out. Theirs' must be gruelling work.

I called for the Moon-goddess to come and charm the weary World, and to bring some joy into his miserable existence. Then called the Chariot to come and soothe the exhausted bank official. We joined emotionally as comforters and friends sharing the harmony. We loved on a spiritual plane, a sort of love I had never experienced before.

Before returning to the beach I said, "Take me to the Empress; I am in pain, my lower tibias are still not healed."

She received us with warmth. Plucking fresh fragrant roses from her garden she said, "You need oil of roses." After preparing the lotion, she rubbed it on both my legs and at the same time withdrew the pain. Then she applied bandages of cream muslin.

As usual, she sent my pain to the Fool to be buried.

Suleman accompanied me to the cave, where I rejoined my meditating earthly body.

Date of meditation: 10/9/91

THE HEAVENLY UNICORN

I lay very still on the transparent wings of meditation and drifted into the inner world; succeeding in suppressing my ego as I crossed the invisible boundary which divides the astral and physical planes.

I looked for Zalmné by the pool but he was nowhere to be found. I took the path to the beach, where I found two unicorns romping, supreme and mystical. I have come to accept their presence in the profound meditation. They are a part of me in the inner-search. Their strength and rare beauty form part of the perfect symmetry of the astral world. They exude a serenity that envelops everything around them. I was transfixed, and I felt I had at last achieved the highest point of self-realisation. It was as if they were the last piece in a jigsaw puzzle; the picture was complete.

Suleman appeared and joined me in my deep contemplation. We stood together holding hands, staring into the blue waters. Suddenly, the sea was swirling. around us. It rose and thrashed against us. I screamed, "Help me, help me!" Suleman grabbed me and I clung to him in terror.

Just as suddenly the sea stilled. A unicorn had spread its wings over us protectively and the sea was calmed. We mounted the unicorn and flew far out into space. I looked back and saw the earth. It was fabulously beautiful.

We returned and landed close by the World-Humanoid. He had taken the form of an African warrior. He appeared to be about thirty six, with a muscular body and smooth glistening skin. He wore a brief loincloth and a striking necklace. On it were charms made from an eagle's claw, a crocodile's tooth, a small green snake. I asked for a gift.

He produced a delicate ivory bracelet patterned with fine petals. I reached out to take it, but as I did he withdrew his outstretched hand, and offered his other hand in which he held a bracelet of silver. I was amazed, it was one I had lost many years ago. He asked, "Would you like this instead?" I took it from him gladly. It was not valuable but it had a strong sentimental attachment to it.

He said, "Wear your long-lost bracelet, it will make you more aware of the power within you."

The Wheel of Fortune joined us. He was still dressed as a bank official, but he seemed fresher and happier. He smiled at me, and I returned his smile. Then I said, "Can I have a gift?"

He answered, "I hold here a precious blue diamond, which I will give to you. Within each facet is an extraordinary power. When the white light of the kundalini within you merges with its blue light, you will unite with another spirit. I know you are worried about your financial security. Do not worry about it, these are earthly concerns and will in time be left behind."

Suleman and I descended to the inner-world from the higher plane of learning. Zalmné was waiting for me patiently. He grabbed my right hand and pulled me onto his stallion. We galloped along the beach, against a cool and bracing sea-wind. I shivered and felt light-hearted after my experience on the upper plane.

I revelled in the freedom of my new enlightenment. Peace and contentment filled my heart. I was glad to be with my guides. I have surrendered myself into their hands.

We galloped to the Chariot's cave. This time it radiated with an emerald glow. She welcomed us warmly and lay me on her healing couch. She pampered my body; massaging and soothing it with a green oil made from forest herbs. Afterwards, I felt relaxed. The journey to the upper plane had drained me and I was exhausted. We headed for the cave and at the clearing we said farewell. I entered the dim shadowy light and rejoined my physical form.

Date of meditation: 16/9/91

A PERSONAL REFLECTION

I am now approaching the end of first year of meditation. It has taught me many skills. I now realise the real meaning of love. My understanding is no longer superficial. I have learnt not to injure others with harsh or cruel words. Even a small insect has a complex existence; which must be respected. After death, it too is spiritually revived in the astral dimension.

I have come to realise the physical aspect of making love is brief and explosive; hardly comparable with the satisfying spiritual love. Bodily orgasm is short, transient, fulfilling for the moment. The pleasure in God's love remains forever: Contentment and bliss mingle to create a divine ecstasy.

I have come to a point in self-realisation where I can be in touch with my God, who is within me. Though my body will return to dust, I will re-awaken with the full-knowledge that I have found the golden casket hidden under the spiritual-road. I know a heavenly treasure awaits me in the kingdom of God.

Now I must collate the knowledge I have gained from my inner guides and the twenty-two archetypes. I will continue on my journey. I hope you will take the same path and share in the love of God and the joy of living.

So rest now in the gentleness of love and open your hearts to receive the spiritual wisdom which is forever yours.

Date of writing: 16/9/91

THE HEALING

I went to meet my guide at the pool. He was sat on his white stallion, waiting for me. He stretched his hand and pulled me up. I held on tightly. His hard muscles rippled under my touch. I rested my cheek against his silky hair. Then I noticed his feet were bare. His mood was light and buoyant, which was unusual.

We talked and without any undue emphasis I said, "I feel restless." As we neared Suleman's cavern I saw he was not alone. A woman was kneeling with her hands clasped in prayer.

We waited. The lady arose first and introduced herself saying, "My name is Isabella and I am your fourth guide."

Suddenly memory flooded in and I remembered the last time I saw her, she was on horseback. Then neither she or Suleman had acknowledged me.

Isabella and I walked along the beach. I could not think of anything to say - my mind had gone blank. We were silent for a long while and I listened to the sighing whispering sea and a cacophonous bird-sound. Eventually I broke our silence by saying, "Could I meet the archetypes who rule my personal relationships?"

She took me to the court of the inner-world. The Justice presided. The golden scales were by his side. The Empress sat on the right of the bench. The World took his place on the left, and from his briefcase, took the documents wherein were recorded the affairs of men. The Shadow arrived with her stag and remained standing. Isabella and I sat down and waited. The Justice waved his hand. I stood up and said, "I have come here for your help, guidance and judgement. I wish to sort out my personal life. I have already received much knowledge from all the archetypes on the spiritual level, but I am unfulfilled as a woman." Everyone stared at me in amazement. I continued, "What I would really like is a sincere man to share my life. I would be glad to have your assistance in this matter."

The archetypes put their heads together and held a brief discussion; then the Justice spoke, "We will help you. In return we ask that you remain in perfect balance with yourself and weigh each action every day truthfully and consciously. Return to this court, when you have found your true happiness."

When we came out, I asked my Shadow, "What is it you want from me to achieve?"

She replied, "Fast in remembrance of me on Wednesdays. This way I will be within you, and your worldly problems will be resolved."

Isabella, my Shadow and I returned to the beach. We stood calmly on the shore. I bade leave and went to the pool.

Zalmné accompanied me to the Chariot's cavern. A pellucid yellow light was glowing within. I went inside, stripped and lay on the couch. She massaged me, soothing the aching discomfort in both my lower tibia bones. She placed hot towels on the painful areas. Then we relaxed in the steaming brook. Its warmth eased my discomfort.

After the healing, we walked towards my cave. Saying farewell, I stepped inside and entered my body.

Date of meditation: 22/9/91

THE EXHILARATION

I went to the pool. Zalmné was not to be seen, so I took the path leading to the beach. When I stood on the shore, an invisible hand picked me up roughly and hurled me into the depths and held me under. I was struggling and fighting for breath under the dark water. I was spluttering and gasping. Some unknown entity was drowning me. Then I felt other hands grasping me, and was propelled upwards into the air. I took a breath and was instantly revived. Zalmné and Suleman took me back to the safety of dry land, and gently lay me on the sand. Zalmné said, "You have been attacked by a demon."

Slowly, the horror of it subsided, leaving me feeling peculiarly lethargic. An oppressive blackness swirled around me.

I put on my green dress and instantly I was refreshed. The cool sea-wind blew around me. Zalmné helped me onto his stallion and then sitting behind me, he took me racing along the shore. He knew I enjoyed this; I love to feel the wind through my hair and to hear the horse's hooves pounding hard and fast. We travelled mile after mile, then abruptly he reined in, coming to a dead-halt. We dismounted and sat and talked. He knew that lately, I was finding it difficult to concentrate when meditating.

My ego persisted in disrupting my thoughts. Zalmné said, "When the Moon is full as it is today, all life forms are affected. Just as the Moon creates tides, it disturbs the psyche."

He continued, "Several factors are responsible for the problems you are experiencing, not just the full moon. The Autumn equinox and your menses also cause disruption. I will summon the High Priestess and the Moon-goddess; so they can help you."

He called them and they emerged from the mistiness of the inner sphere. We stood in a straight line on the beach. There was a bright moon shining in the silver sky. The High Priestess looked up staring at it transfixed in enchantment. I stood beside her, equally enraptured in wonder. The Moon-goddess appeared to be communing with the bright heavenly body. There was a look of sheer delight on her face.

As I looked into the face of the High Priestess, I have never seen such radiant beauty. She was drawing on the Moon's light and transferring it to my third eye. I felt its power surging within me.

As I searched the silvery sky, I saw a moon spirit floating in the fiery fluorescence, then an air spirit eddied in the eerie translucence, and a luminous water spirit shimmered over the waves, gliding like a shadowy phantom.

I was enthralled in their loveliness. The three of us joined hands and together we danced.

Later after I had left the Moon-goddess and the High Priestess, I returned with Zalmné to Suleman's beach. I asked them why I felt sick in the deep meditation.

Zalmné answered, "The kundalini power is awakening. To alleviate the discomfort, bathe often in the salty sea-water, or relax in the bath of herbal salts."

Then we walked towards the cave and after saying farewell I rejoined my body sitting upright in bed waiting for my return.

Date of meditation: 23/9/91 8.00-8.45 AM

THE WHITE LIGHT

With great difficulty and a considerable amount of concentration I arrived at the pool. Since the onset of the Autumn equinox and the full moon, the inner world's imagery has been hazy and weak. Zalmné had explained the causes of the magnetic interference. After trying really hard I succeeded in overcoming the problem and I was free-floating in the astral-space.

I fetched my green dress and put it on. Miraculously the sphere became even more luminescent. Zalmné was not at the pool, so I went to the beach. I stood near the sea listening to the waves. The fresh breeze tickled my skin making me shiver. Isabella appeared. Her large shape silhouetted against the misty sky.

I was glad to see her; I liked her. She was gentle and serene and a perpetual soft smile enhanced her face. She was not particularly beautiful but pleasant to look at, and her eyes shone with a radiant light. A bright and reflective aura surrounded her heavy frame. I spoke first, "Please call all the feminine archetypes to come and join us. I want to feel their love."

She transmitted her message across the inner-space and all the ladies assembled on the beach. They were dressed as before except the High Priestess. She wore a long shimmering gown, encrusted with gems and decorated with mysterious symbols.

I revelled in their presence and their love. In return I gave them mine. Then we all went in search of my Shadow. We went deeper and deeper into the green forest and at last I caught sight of her, sitting astride her stag hidden by the green shadows. The stag, startled by our rustling darted back into the dense vegetation and disappeared.

The Chariot and the Moon-goddess left us. The High Priestess and Isabella accompanied me to find the Sun-Humanoid. When at last we traced him, I said, "I have seen you as a sun-spirit and a sun-angel, but not yet as a humanoid."

No sooner had I spoken then he transformed into a humanoid. I looked above to the glistening sky and to my astonishment I saw a pale yellow stallion descending. Seated on it was a man. He looked strong, masculine and dignified. He was attractive with loose flowing blonde wavy hair falling to his knees. He was draped in a. transparent pale-lemon chiffon material. It fluttered in the breeze as the stallion came and landed on the beach.

The man had a perfect physique complementing his striking good looks. He was carrying a crystal sword in each hand. They gleamed and dazzled in the golden rays of the sun as he waved them. The whole inner-sky blazed with rainbow reflections. I stared at the apparition stupefied.

He did not speak and without forewarning he raised his right hand and thrust the sword deep into my third eye. It passed through me and protruded from the back of my head. Strangely, there was no pain. I seemed to be drifting in a white light.

My attacker withdrew the crystal sword from my third eye, and pulled me up behind him. The rhythmic movement of yellow stallion became sensually, erotic. We rode together for a while, then he suddenly reigned his mount and we dismounted to lay on the grass, where we united in unbridled passion. We lay on the cool grass under the canopy of the tall trees. We made love tempestuously, ardently. The resulting pleasure was almost beyond belief. It was beautiful and totally fulfilled our every spiritual and physical desire.

Afterwards, I found Isabella and we returned to the beach. I said calmly, "I am wholly fulfilled." To my surprise Isabella gave no explanation for the encounter I had experienced. I said farewell and I returned to the physical world.

Date of meditation: 29/9/91 7.00 AM.

THE WHITE LIGHTNING

Zalmné was waiting for me by the pool. Immediately I noticed the feathers on his head-dress were all in black and white! I was intrigued and questioned, "Why do you wear only black and white feathers?"

He answered promptly, "Black is the colour of the earth and white belongs to heaven. " He did not elaborate!

Then to my amazement, I saw my four bodies drifting in the astral dimension looking exactly like me.

Zalmné explained, "Your earth body lives in the physical world. Your fire body explores the spiritual. Your water body is emotional and reflective, and your air body is engrossed in time and mind."

I realised I was fortunate in coming this far. Guided by unseen power. I would not have done so on my own. I would have lost my way in the darkness.

Then I said, "Take me to the Empress I want her advice on a worldly problem. "

We floated through the dimension to her palace. When I saw her I said, "What does the future hold for me ?"

She advised, "You have much to accomplish. Be brave and bear the traumas of life. For soon, every piece will fit like the jigsaw puzzle."

Then in the space of my mind in the area of my third eye, I saw an eye appear out of the swirling mists. It was guiding me to an electric-blue light. I asked, "Where are we?"

Zalmné replied, "You are in the zone of your deep mind. Go back in time and bring this memory to the fore."

I remembered and the past flooded in. I was restful and tranquil just after the pre-op injection. Then I happened to glance across to the huge hospital windows. To my surprise I saw white flashes of lightning, but I heard no thunder, puzzled, I pushed it into the unconscious and over the years forgot about it. Now many years later I was being made conscious of it by my guide.

"What was the lightning?" I asked. I was unprepared for his reply. "It was

HIGH PRIESTESS

the kundalini lightning you saw. You will remember, your life changed from that moment on. You were alerted to the mysterious power you could not figure it out all by yourself. That is why, by your meditation you have contacted the inner guides. The purpose of our existence is to guide you along your inner-path and to help you as much as possible."

I confided, "Sometimes, the interaction of the powerful archetypes causes aches and pains in my physical body."

"Information received from the archetypes is occasionally too much for the psyche to cope with." he explained, "I am here to alleviate any discomfort you suffer from. You have arrived at the culmination of your life, where the self is able to accumulate knowledge, assimilate wisdom accurately, collate perspective ideas and actions relative to it. You must discard that which is useless to function on a higher level of reality."

I was quite happy with his profound statement, and I retraced my steps joyfully back to my other body.

Date of meditation: 8/10/91   12:46 - 1.27 PM

SPHERES OF GEBURAH AND CHESED

INVISIBLE DEATH

I found the inner cave and followed the dove to the pool. 'The astral-landscape was clear and colourful. Zalmné was not there to greet me, so I strolled leisurely on the path leading to the beach.

It was deserted; there was not a soul or bird to be seen. I looked for Suleman in the crystal cave but he was absent. I called Isabella, without any response. In desperation, I called King Solomon

I gazed in the blue sky scanning the horizon. In the far distance a golden chariot was descending gradually. I saw the bright metal gleaming in the sunshine. It was pulled by four white-winged stallions. It landed near me and I saw King Solomon.

He stepped out. I noticed his long satin shirt reached his ankles. It was imprinted with fine sky blue vertical stripes. His jet black hair, loose and wispy, falling half-way down his back complemented his dark beard. His large sapphire blazed in the sunlight, enhancing his deep-blue eyes which twinkled in merriment. His whole body was surrounded by a glowing heavenly light.

I took his hand shyly and we stood like this for a long time , staring out to sea in inward contemplation. My thoughts immediately turned to God.
I asked, "Can you explain God's mystery?"

He answered without any hesitation, "Heaven is huge, it has countless numbers of precious gems scattered over its lands, bigger than any on the earth. God's existence is a timeless existence. It can create and destroy all complex life-forms. It is, has been and forever will be."

He continued to expound, "God is the eternity, the master of time, space and matter. Seen and unseen. By his enormous calculations we have come into being. He has sculptured lands into living spheres so that we can learn of his immense love. His radiance shines in our hearts and in the golden sunsets glimmering on the distant shores.

With the seed of love planted in our hearts, man may awaken from the mother's womb to take their station in life. With wisdom in his soul and food in his belly, he traverses the plains of the world, yet still he is half asleep. He partakes of the beauty half-awakened! If only Mankind listened to the voice within. He will truly rise to a blissful dawn, like the bird which sings a merry song to greet each new day."

I was still standing on the beach in a daze and I felt alone. I thought where has my guide gone? In uncontrolled panic I struggled. Something opaque swirled around me and I became giddy and faint! The next moment I was drifting through black space. I became afraid and gasped for breath! Somehow, I sensed I was in the Abyss and I thought I was going to die! Miraculously, Zalmné appeared beside me and pulled me away from the grip of this particular torment.

I asked him sombrely, "Why was I left alone?"

"No guide can go with you beyond a certain point," he replied. "You have to experience the 'invisible wings of death' by yourself. You are now in the spheres of Geburah and Chesed in the Mystic Realm."

We returned to the tranquil Autumn pool and I was divinely happy. As I lay resting in the water I had a vision.

A man appeared on a black stallion incredibly masculine and strong. He was dressed in a white flowing robe and a mystical veil shielded his face. A gold band encircled his brow encrusted with heavenly jewels. The veil was transparent and light. Within it I perceived the beauty of his face. A voice said unto me, "You have seen God."

"Why me?" I asked.

"Because you seek me with your love." He replied.

My inner voice communed with him. I was in love with all humanity; spring blossoms and autumn berries, flaming sun and radiant moon, with God and my soul.

The vision ended. I descended from the Mystic Realm and returned once-more to my material world.

Date of meditation: 9/10/91   600-7.00 AM

THE MASCULINE SHADOW

I had difficulty in getting in to the inner world The visual perceptions were weak, but with intense concentration, I was able to be free of the ego's grip, thoughts and feelings.

I was standing at the Spring pool and I called for Zalmné to come. He did not respond so I walked in the short secret tunnel leading to the Autumn pool, but alas, he was nowhere to be seen and the astral landscape was unusually quiet. I noticed the fire had been lit and the amber flames flickered, fanned by the brisk breeze. I observed the chestnut mare grazing peacefully, oblivious of my presence. The solitude was blissful and restful. I fetched my green dress and put it on. Unexpectedly, I saw my guide Zalmné standing akin to a statue across the other side of the pool. His aura shimmered, it was bright but mystifying, shrouded in a spirit-substance, transparent and luminary in the mystical transformation.

The white flimsy chiffon draped around him, hugging his masculine body. He stood in a contemplation with legs apart and arms outstretched to the sky. His silky black hair blown by the blustery breeze.

I watched him for a long time, in his pose of trance and meditation. Then he noticed me and beckoned for me to go over. He helped me onto his white stallion.

He raced on the plains of the inner dimension, moving further away from the familiar land. He stopped. We dismounted and walked in the wilderness by foot.

Taking hold of my right hand he said, "Come with me, I will show you the power-lioness." I travelled progressively deeper into the zone of deep mind and with his shamanism he transformed me into a lioness.

I was hunting in the dry bracken. Pangs of hunger rumbling in my belly. Instincts were aroused. The pungent smell of prey eddied on the current of air. Crouched, hidden in the brittle fern I watched a fawn. I followed its every movement, then I pounced! I missed! The animal scrambled and darted off frightened and squealing.

I continued on my journey under a canopy of the tall-trees, amidst a cacophonous sounds of the birds and the monkeys, the buzzing insects biting my skin, annoying me. I swished my tufted tail to get rid of them!

Finally, I arrived at my destination. My pride of lions lolling and lazing around. My two cubs darted towards me in fondness and greeting. I nuzzled them in affection and lay on the ground to fondle and play with them licking their soft fur with love and devotion.

Then the power-lioness faded and receded from the zone of the deep mind. I lost touch with her and she vanished from sight. My guide and I were still standing amongst the lions but I was not afraid as he was with me. I have come to trust his profound knowledge completely.

At this point I saw a young man reclining on a fallen tree-trunk. I was surprised to see him and stared at him in fascination, especially at his feet! For some reason, I found them very attractive. His legs were long and smooth with glistening skin, and his hair was long and silky-black, similar to Zalmné's. He looked about seventeen, and seemed to be perfectly at ease while surrounded by the lions. They did not appear to bother him at all!

I enquired, "Who are you?"

He replied, "I am your masculine Shadow." I was shocked! Zalmné had not prepared me for this encounter, not even a faint glimmer of intuition or precognition had entered my mind. I said to myself, well, even the inner world is full of surprises and wonder!

The youth was kind, his mood light and his smile bright. I liked him, and stayed with him for a while, enjoying the companionship. I could not think of anything to say to him, and he, as if sensing this left me pondering in my silence.

My guide and I retreated from the deep inner-mind reflection and once more returned to the pool. We sat down and contemplated by its quiet waters.

Shortly we left for the Chariot's cavern. Once arriving there I relaxed in the warm bubbling-brook. Its properties purified me and rid me of the aches and pains in my body. The Star-Alien come and joined us and we enjoyed the companionship of being together.

My guide and I went to my cave, whereupon we said farewell, and I went back into my own physical body.

Date of meditation: 12/10/91   7:15 - 8:35 AM

THE SEA OF TRANQUILLITY.

Without any bother I was transported to the inner world. The ego was perceptibly quiet, barely audible; not filling my head with gibberish nonsense. The visual images came fast and clear

I was beside the pool but Zalmné was absent. Instead, I observed several white animals. I was intrigued. Why all white? Nevertheless, I admired the tremendous beauty and serenity of it all. At the same time, my intuition was stirring deeply inside me.

My green dress was blowing in the wind. I fetched it and put it on. Then I lay down in the hammock, waiting for Zalmné to come. I waited a fair while, but he did not appear, neither did he respond to my call. The swaying motion and gentle rhythm of the hammock instilled in me a peacefulness and dawning realisation of contentment. I wanted to remain in this state forever, but slowly, with much deliberation, I raised myself lazily out of this reverie to go and look for a guide.

I saw my dove perched up a tree. I commanded it, and it flew on to the beach. When I reached the beach, I called Suleman, without any response.
I thought that he must be busy on the other planes.

Next I summoned Isabella, and immediately she came into view, calmly staring out to sea in contemplation. I saw that she was dressed differently, wearing an attire similar to a nun's habit, in a dark grey tweed material with white cotton cuffs and a white veil pulled neatly over her head.

I stretched out my right hand in greeting and she clasped it, I felt a tingly electric sensation suffusing my whole body. I took my hand away quickly.

The love between us had blossomed and bonded perfectly together by the pebble's power. Once again we held hands tightly as we strolled leisurely on the shore. The breaking waves soothed my feet and it pleased me to see my foot-prints patterned the smooth sand.

Isabella took me near the shore and guided me into the frothy gushing waters. We were submerged up to the neck. Then I saw a sleeping apparition hovering before us. The sea became calm and transluscent blue. The sky filled with silver-white. The figure awakened and said, "I am the Spirit." At this point all my senses, chakras and higher-self opened to commune with the spectre.

The ghostly person continued, "I am the White Light which you have been experiencing and seeing in your meditational journey. You are a human-being searching on your spiritual path and one who seeks will receive; and that where love is there is never any segregation. The white light shines for you now but soon it will come to all."

I was profoundly elated by seeing the transparent white light. Isabella and I came out of the cool blue sea and rested on the golden sands to be warmed in the sun.

Then we walked a long way then I broke the pleasant silence. "Can you bring the Empress. I would like to be with her to feel her love." Isabella summoned her by a mysterious telepathy. When she arrived immediatly she transferred her pure loving into my heart. I held her right hand and Isabella's left. On contact their power was strong. I was drained of all my worldly emotion and I was cleansed of any impurity. The Empress left us and Isabella and I continued to walk across the sands towards the Autumn pool. When we reached the pool I stepped into the cool waters and Isabella bathed my brow. I relaxed, it was good and refreshing. The hours passed but Zalmné did not come to the pool. I hugged Isabella before I left and returned to my worldly body.

Date of meditation: 13/10/91 8:27-8:50

MYSTERY OF THE INNER-HEALING

THE FOUR BODIES

I contacted Zalmné at the Autumn pool. It was fairly difficult to remain in the meditation-state. The ego persisted with its own peculiar insistence; interfering and bringing to the fore all the unnecessary worries of the physical world.

My guide was squatting by the pool, dressed in a traditional costume. His hair combed straight back, held in the nape of his neck by coloured beads. A white eagle was perched on his shoulder.

I complained, "I can't relate properly to the inner world." He stared at me and said, "Go and put on your green dress."

I changed and was immediately touched by the inner-breeze. Shivers tingled on my spine.

We talked together.

Out of the blue I questioned, "Who are my Four Bodies?"

Zalmné replied, "The earth-ego moves on the material plane. The fire-spiritual in the domain of the soul. The water-emotional is the love within and the air-mental explores the realm of the alien."

It made sense. After seeing the four aspects of myself I marvelled at the momentous significance.

He commented, "Now that you have seen the four bodies, you will begin to balance."

"Why have I not yet seen the exploding white light?"

"I am regulating the kundalini and slowly it is being released into the self. Sudden exposure to the white light is harmful to the psyche. For now, you are learning its secret wisdom. What you have seen and been told of the inner world must be written; for others to gain knowledge to enable them to follow this path."

The deep meditation had left me feeling lethargic so we went to see the Chariot. Today, her cavern was suffused with a brilliant white glow. I stepped inside; my guide waited outside. I lay down on the couch. She placed her cool hands on me and massaged fragrant oil of jasmine all over. I relaxed and was refreshed.

I did not want to return to my outside world. It is so peaceful being here and the observation of my Four Selves had left me glowing with inner-contentment.

I was really reluctant to leave and my guide remarked, "You have to go back. I will accompany you to the cave."

We said farewell, I stepped inside and returned to my still body.

Date of meditation: 14/10/91 10:00-10.30 AM

THE ARCHETYPAL IMBALANCE

In the darkness of my mind I saw the cave etched against the inner landscape.

I stepped in it, touching the wall to the left of me and I was once more in the astral world. I searched at both the pools for Zalmné, but he was not around, so I followed my spiritual dove, to the beach.

I scanned the beach for Suleman but he did not come into view. In the distance there was a black stallion coming nearer. As it galloped closer I realised the man on it was King Solomon. His visage was radiant and his aura shimmered in a heavenly silver light.

He dressed like a nomad and the blue sapphire gleamed in the yellow sunlight. I could not decide which was the more appealing. His sparkling blue eyes or the sapphire. Nothing specific came to mind to question. Only that his love was transmitting freely transferring to my inner-self flowing into my heart. All that I wanted was to share in his bountiful love. After filling my soul with his offered love, I said, "Call the High Priestess, I want her psychic power to penetrate my being."

When she arrived she was magnificently attired. Seated very erect and elegant on her grey-flecked mare. Her shining gown enhanced by glittering jewels. Some of the stones I had never seen before. Her crown was cast in platinum gold and exquisitely engraved with droplets of white lustrous pearls all around the circumference. Large peacock feathers plumed from the centre and downy feathers were sewn on her royal blue satin robe.

She gave me her psychic power at the same time saying, "I will be with you directing you."

I said to King Solomon, "Bring me my unconscious self, I want to find the cause of my alienation, to seek out the archetype responsible for this dilemma."

The World, being the culprit was brought forward. He was in the same attire as before. The Emperor arrived next and he was encloaked in a heavy scarlet and orange satin robe.

As soon as these two met I sensed the hostility coursing through them. They argued and bickered.

"Saturn," I said, "will you give me your advice on how to deal with anger?"

"The Emperor is responsible deep within the unconscious. He is responsible for this in your exterior world. Follow this procedure and the smouldering anger will dissipate. Run cold water over your hands and wrists then touch your brow with the coolness."

The Emperor became angry on hearing these words. It was evident the archetypes were not in harmony. I asked them to co-operate and work in harmony and unity. They promised to be more friendly and duly left.

I was left wondering, why my alienation had not been discussed? I had not pressed for an answer. Perhaps, that would come later on.

I was wearied by the World and Emperor archetypes Their constant disagreements had drained me and I had not been prepared for this.

We walked to the Chariot's abode. Her greeting was warm and friendly. It seems all the feminine archetypes are in perfect balance with each other. I was inwardly pleased about this. I liked them all. They have given me so much conviviality; the High Priestess had even imparted some of her profound wisdom.

The High Priestess left us mysteriously. The Chariot and I bathed in the warm bubbling natural waters . We enjoyed each other's company. The prevailing solitude touched and gladdened my spirit.

My guide rode with me to the edge of the forest. He left me at the entrance to the cave. I returned to my still body.

Date of meditation: 20/10/91 9:09 - 9.40 PM

DETACHMENT OF THE EGO

There was a lot of difficulty in entering the inner world. A darkness curtained my mind. The ego at its maximum force would not relinquish its hold. There were several noises in the background; which made it harder to concentrate on the perceptions of the astral dimension.

I was aware of the radiators banging and cracking loudly! The ticking of the clock over-amplified; and the traffic on the busy road outside grinding on my nerves.

With deep breathing and rhythmic motion of the mental triangle I projected onto the mind's screen; I was able to be free of the ego's thought-manipulations; and I was standing inside the dimly lit cave. I could not move forward. I seemed to be glued to the spot. I called for a guide, "Help me, help me!" I was aware of two hands coming out of the darkness to my assistance. They grabbed me and pulled me onto the inner-landscape.

I was at the Autumn pool and Zalmné was beside me. His hair was parted in the middle and hung in two long plaits resting on each breast-bone. He was attired in the traditional Red-Indian clothes, but without any feathers or finery

My head was whizzing round with questions. Yet none would come to the fore in any clarity. It was all mumbo-jumbo. Suddenly, I blurted out, "Why do you never answer my questions directly?"

He answered, "You could not understand. Although you cannot see me in the physical world, I do exist for you in the astral. You locate me by your inner-search. I am like the dust floating in the sunlight: When your radiance shines on me, I become alive and by the quest of your meditation, I live for you."

I said, "Give me your advice on a personal problem. F has asked for my house-key so he can come and go as he pleases."

His reply was prompt and decisive. "A key is a rare possession. Treasure it and keep it near to your heart. To part with it unnecessarily invites discord. At the present moment it would not be a wise decision for you to let him have the key."

I questioned him further about my alienation? He responded, "It is a necessary function for the present time. You are on the road of self-awareness, on the path you have chosen. Your life has to remain simple to achieve what you have undertaken."

I said, "I am loathe to get rid of my car. It is a painful transition. What shall I do?"

He answered straightaway, "It is the fault of your ego, it receives much pleasure from owning material possessions. When the car is finally sold it will suffer much pain. The ego remains incessantly tied, craving for materialism."

"I will find it terribly difficult to sell the car?"

"Detachment from the material self is not easy to do. The ego is the cause of much heartache."

I put forward another question. "Why have I worked with so many guides so soon?"

"You were ready for in-depth exploration. It is better you work with us this way. I realise our bond is strong and special, and I will never leave you. I will remain in the background. Working with the other guides as well, the guidance can be taught at a much faster pace." My love for Zalmné surged within me; the passion truly awakened.

I remarked, "I must leave you now. I have to go and write, otherwise I will forget our discourse as it recedes back into the unconscious."

I retreated from the inner world and returned to unite with my barely-breathing body, sitting still in bed in meditation.

Date of meditation: 26/10/91 6:55 - 7:48 AM

SPHERE OF BINAH

THE ELUSIVE MYSTERIES

I neared the pool and beloved Zalmné was waiting for me patiently. I saw the unicorn, a cow and an ox. They were all white.

I straddled his powerful stallion, behind him. We went to the beach. I looked above to the sky and saw Suleman slowly descending on his unicorn. He landed on the white beach shrouded in a white haze. He wore a pale pink chemise which was lustrous in the misty light. His turban and sash were in a shade of deep purple. A large flashing diamond in the middle of his forehead blazed with blue fire.

Zalmné mysteriously vanished. We were alone on the sea-shore. I complimented him saying, "You look truly divine."

I continued, "Can you explain the mystery of the crop circles?"

"It is a sign from God," he answered, "the earth is speaking to us!"

Take heed oh you foolish men,
Do not destroy the magnificence.
Kill not the beast of the forest,
Or the fish in the sea.

"Take me to my Shadow." I duly said, after the sadness slowly subsided.

We trekked through the forest and then I saw her astride her mystical stag. I said, "I have not been able to fulfil my promise to you to fast on Wednesdays."

"Never mind," she said gently.

Then I saw a man wearing a white lengthy veil over his head and eyes. It reached to his waist and was held in place by a black velvet band all around his forehead. He came nearer and suddenly it dawned on me it was King Solomon! Suleman mysteriously vanished.

King Solomon and I returned to the beach. Out of his scabbard he withdrew a gleaming silver sword and with its mystical power slashed the sky! At this command the clouds parted and we were drifting in a serene white light. Then we floated in a tunnel of extreme blue brightness. Dumbfounded, I asked, "Where are we?" He replied, "You are in the Sphere of Binah."

I saw the angel of Binah with her lotus shaped crown and her beautiful sparkling eyes. I moaned, "The power of Binah is excruciating, my psyche cannot take it much longer, I have to leave!'

We went to visit the Chariot. Today her cavern was lit by an emerald light. I stepped inside and hugged her. The tension evaporated as she proceeded to heal the discomfort and heaviness in my body. I sat down on the couch and she embraced me. We were united in a complete understanding, total bliss and harmony.

King Solomon accompanied me to the cave. We said farewell at the clearing. I stepped into the dim shadowy light and in my body. As soon as I returned, I noticed: the pain near the womb-area had lessened. I had been suffering terribly with it for several days. The Chariot's unique healing had taken a profound effect!

Date of meditation: 1/11/91

EMPRESS

OLD PAN

THE HEALING COMMUNION

Today when I reached the inner world; the sphere was picturesque and lucid. Zalmné was not at the Autumn pool so I carried on to the beach. As soon as I saw Isabella I mentioned, "I am still suffering from nagging aches and pains." By her miraculous power she separated my four bodies and sent the earth-body to the Chariot's cavern.

She greeted me with affection and we bathed in the natural bubbling water. The warmth penetrated my abdomen. Various coloured crystals were placed on my stomach and lower spine. An icy-coldness gripped at my insides. Then she parted my legs, put her hand in my vagina and touched my womb with a healing crystal.

After the healing was over; Isabella and I searched for my Shadow. Eventually we found her accompanied by her mystical stag. At once, I was attracted to her wild beauty. I reached out and touched the animal with my right hand. My Shadow said, "Come and sit with me ." In joy I responded. I clambered on the creature clumsily, put my arms around her waist and hugged her. Unusual sensations empowered my body; like a sort of electrical-tingling vibrating through me. I apologised to her, "Sorry, for not keeping the fast on Wednesdays, but I have been feeling ill with my menses."

"It does not matter," she responded kindly. "I know many avenues are difficult for you. Think of me when you can, I will understand."

The three of us went to the Autumn pool and as soon as Zalmné appeared on the scene, Isabella and the Shadow vanished, like ghosts disappearing, silently and effortlessly.

My guide and I did not speak at first. We were silent for a long time just savouring the companionship; especially me, I loved to be with him. I said, "Transfer my consciousness. I want to be on the plane of the dreaming and waking realm; where I am aware of this world and the astral both at the same time."

Zalmné induced me by his hypnotic powers, so to transfer me to the hypnotised state.

In this strange place, I was extremely light-hearted and jubilant, riding with him astride his stallion. We travelled a fair distance and then on the bank of a swollen river he stopped.

The air was light, clean and fresh. The atmosphere cool, calm and crisp. It seemed as if we were in a sort of haven.

I noticed a narrow concrete ledge about two feet wide crossing the huge expanse of the turbulent river. The currents flowed fast and ferocious. Zalmné gesticulated, "We are going across, don't be afraid, you will experience much fear, but it will be for the good."

The stallion advanced carefully. I was petrified! I clung to my guide in terror! At best of times I did not like masses of water. I was frightened and elated at the same time. A concoction of emotion swept over me.

We were half-way, when suddenly and unexplainably a grace possessed my very soul submerging me in its immense depth. I was aware of a delightful presence and an enchanting benevolence eddying all around me. I was enmeshed in the rational wonderment. This is what real living should be like, I thought and sighed heavily. It is a pity I have to leave it behind.

As my fear subsided Zalmné aroused me from the hypnotic trance. I did not want to leave this extraordinary esoteric domain of divinity. The beauty is unequalled by any I have seen on earth. I wanted to remain here forever.

Zalmné interrupted my sublime dreaming, "It is enough for now; you must go back to your other world."

Dejected, I came back, knowing the worldly reality was hard to face. I wished the mystical wisdom could remain mine for all time.

Date of meditation: 4/11/91   7.30 AM

THE LOVING

I was meditating. The soft melodious music, Pathways to Love, was playing in the background. The visual perceptions were clear and colourful. As soon as I stepped in the cave, I went over to the entrance opposite and stared at the scene below. The emerald sea and deep blue sky, the green grass swaying in the wind.

I retreated again into the cave and touching the wall on my left transparently moved onto the inner landscape. I stood very still and perused the path. Then I summoned the spiritual dove. It perched on my arm. "Take me to my inner guide," I whispered softly with my inner voice. By now all my senses were fully alert and the images filtered in vivid and fast. I followed the dove flitting between the trees to the Spring pool where I first met my guide.

I was lucky, for I saw him astride his white stallion. I went close to him and touched his bare brown skin on the upper thigh. His leg felt strong, and hard under my palm. He grabbed my hand and pulled me up to sit beside him. I released a soft sigh and rested my cheek against his hard back.

He raced the powerful stallion to the edge of the cliff; stopping at the precipice. I was scared! Heights made me feel dizzy and light-headed. The heady perfume of the fragrant valleys was delightfully pungent and fresh.

I breathed in deeply turning my head towards the breeze carrying the fragrance. The solitude was perfectly sublime.

Suddenly I said, "Take me to the Empress." He turned around and headed towards the palace. I was pleased that the High Priestess and the

Chariot were with the Empress. They greeted me warmly. We joined hands standing in a circle, and the power of their gifts vibrated through me, pulsating in my being.

I was most especially aware of the burning flames in both my palms. The psychic power of the Priestess was in me and the Empress' love was within me, and the Chariot healed the pain in my tibias by massage.

At this point I became aware that all the archetypes were beginning to assemble. They came together one by one. I thought, this is indeed auspicious. Joining hands, they formed a large circle, except the Emperor and World, they were in the middle. I realised at this point, they were here for the appraisal and judgement of their behaviour in my psyche. To fulfil their promise of being friendlier towards each other. I was profoundly aware of the power of the archetypes.

I was seized in the delirious fever of the kundalini. The vivid clarity of inner-truth burned even brighter, and the white light of brilliance expanded everywhere and the divine radiance filling my soul. My guide ordered, "Go and lie in the pool." I floated on the top and the two black mambas slithered on my still body. I felt the kundalini rising in my belly; whilst the crawling mambas moved over my feet, snaking upwards to my thighs, solar plexus and fingertips. I spread my arms wide contemplating and experiencing a sensation of flying through an unknown dimension. Perplexed I asked, "Where am I?"

Zalmné promptly replied, "You are in the Sphere of Binah." Having fed my soul of the beauty of this sphere, I returned to my worldly existence.

Date of meditation: 6/11/91 - 11.20-11.45 AM

MEETING THE FIFTH GUIDE

I went into the inner world hoping to see Zalmné. He was not waiting at our usual place. I fetched the green silk dress and put it on. I carried on walking to the beach to find Isabella. Turning in the direction of Suleman's cave I headed towards it, watching my feet patterning the sand. I sat on a large boulder staring out to sea waiting for a guide to emerge from the astral space.

I pondered what to do next. Beginning to feel lonely and afraid; conscious of the fear spreading within me.

Out of the pellucid light, a man appeared astride a grey-white dappled mare. He wore a pale grey shantung silk turban, one end of it trailed loose over his left shoulder at the front, fluttering wildly in the wind. In the centre of it was a plume of cascading ostrich feathers. His chemise was in a dazzling white chiffon, and tight fitting pants of a heavy satin in the same colour. Mounted on his black leather belt was an ornate scabbard and a dagger bejewelled in sapphires, emeralds and rubies.

He moved towards me but as I was still deep in thought I did not fully acknowledge his presence, thinking that he would just pass by. To my horror he stopped right in front of me and announced, "I am Chindar." I ignored him still trapped in my fear. He did not move on but reiterated, "I am Chindar, your fifth guide." In disbelief I stammered, "Show me some proof."

"Come with me." he said. I was unsure whether to go but slowly and reluctantly I followed him. He took me to an unknown place and we encountered a group sitting around a blazing fire, eating their evening meal.

They had their backs to me and their faces were hidden by dark wide hoods and their bodies covered in heavy black cloaks. "Sit down, come and eat with us," one of them said. In the brightness of the blue fire-light I noticed with mild surprise that the three people were my previous guides. I stared at them unbelievingly. "What is all this about?" I asked. Zalmné answered, "We did not answer your call as you were to meet Chindar." Chindar and I left the threesome; their mysterious silhouettes etched against the starry sky.

We rode towards the beach and on the deserted shore we stood with our hands clasped tightly and talked at length. I questioned, "Where exactly am I at this moment in time?"

He answered straightaway, "You have surpassed the beauty of Tipareth and gone past the Spheres of Geburah and Chesed. You have surmounted the Veil of Lesser Mysteries and encountered the Veil of Greater Mysteries."

"I have not meditated for some time," I sighed and whispered softly. "Every time I tried only obscurity and confusion filled my senses."

He explained, "After the mass exhilaration of the Sephiroth, you needed to rest, so that you could try to solve the even greater mysteries."

Concerned, I asked, "Having known such divine beauty, love and joy in the heart of the Spheres, how am I to exist in my ordinary mortal world?"

He answered, "We do not ask anything specific of you. Your life is for living, and you should not be lonely. Be brave and be true unto yourself. This way you will remain buoyant and exuberant."

I told him without any emotion. "I feel an affinity for you as I do for Zalmné." I held his hand tight and a warm rush of love filled both our hearts.

He squeezed my hand saying, "Zalmné was very special to you. He was your shaman to the inner self, your link to the inner world. As long as you need our love and guidance, none of us will ever leave you. We will commune with you always."

"Why have I met so many guides so soon?" I queried.

"Time is running out," he responded, "we still have much to teach you and you have much to learn to perfect yourself; before you will be ready to meet your Master and Maker. Our purpose is to guide you along your course."

Suddenly, I blurted out, "Where do you come from?"

"I am Chindar, from the heartlands of the Mogul-Raj."

I liked Chindar immensely instantly and knew our love would be strong and deep. On a similar level to my love of Zalmné but profoundly different. As Chindar's personality was light and airy, like the cool summer breeze. Vivacious and effervescent, like champagne. Without meaning to be too inquisitive I said, "Is your home in the inner-world?"

"I roam in the wilds. I have many caves scattered in the wilderness. I am restless, I move here, there and everywhere."

"I must go now," I said.

He offered, "I will take you." He called his stallion and we mounted. At the clearing I enquired anxiously, "Where shall I meet you next time?"

"Just at the edge of the forest." he replied quietly.

I waved to him before I stepped into the cave, then re-entered my body, sitting upright in bed propped by pillows, slumbering in deep-level meditation.

Date of meditation: 6/12/91 8.41-9.18 AM.

SPHERE OF CHOKMA

THE AGONY AND ECSTASY

I was listening to the tape Pathways to love. Straightaway; I was on the secluded beach. The mystical unicorn seemed peaceful. I went over to him and nuzzled his graceful form. Suleman was by the crystal cavern: I studied him. His eyes shone with a heavenly light and his face was radiant. He wore a turban and over his robes, a wide sash in a bright purple chiffon. One end of it trailed over his right shoulder at the front and fluttered in the breeze. His chiffon chemise was a shade of pale pink. I thought he looked really handsome.

He did not speak and we stood together in silent contemplation for a short while. He broke the silence by saying: "Today, I will take you to the Sphere of Chokmah." I did not reply but waited in anticipation, as I had no idea. what to expect.

Suleman summoned the Emperor. He came in all his splendour; in the glorious head-dress of rainbow feathers. He looked proud and dignified. We joined hands and our bond became stronger.

After a short time of resting we set off on our journey to an inner dimension where colourful mists swirled and iridescent rainbows arched over the tree-tops. I was filled with ecstasy as I saw the angel of Chokma.

Afterwards Suleman and I returned to the secluded beach. I didn't stay long as I wanted to record all the details of my experience.

Date of meditation: 17/12/91 11.39-11.51 AM

THE LIFE OF THE DEAD

Today I did not have any trouble in entering the inner world. Straightaway, I found myself at the pool. I did not see Zalmné immediately; sometimes in the inner dimension the ego upsurges to play havoc and prevents my concentration. When he did come into my vision, he seemed like a ghostly spectre, as he came galloping towards me on his white stallion. When he came within reach, he took a hand and pulled me up to behind him. His silky hair brushed my cheek and I held on tightly around his waist resting my face against his hard back.

When we dismounted, I ran my eyes over his bare upper-half searching for any unusual marks. I saw a small brown mole on his left nipple.

Suddenly, without any warning I saw Ayaz my nephew who had died in a car accident. I was puzzled, and could not understand why he should appear here. He was smiling, and appeared at peace. I cried, and between sobs, I saw my earthly father. After my sadness had been washed away I asked, "Why did I see them?"

My guide replied, "The spirits of the dead shall be remembered. It is by remembrance of them through prayers and lamentations that their sins shall be absolved."

Then we went to visit the Empress. I wanted to feel her love in my psyche. She was dressed in a bright yellow flimsy chiffon gown. A sort of plume of cascading feathers was attached to her crown. As soon as I saw her; I felt love surging within me. Our souls entwined in frenzied delirium, spiritually mingling and reaching out to the stars. The contentment was serene and satisfying, fulfilling our every wish and desire.

After this psychic union I felt our bond had been strengthened. I was happy and exuberant this was so.

After saying farewell to my guide at the clearing I stepped into the cool dark cave and into my own body.

Date of meditation: 18/12/91

INNER FULFILMENT

I must have tried for at least fifteen minutes before I finally succeeded in locating the Autumn pool. I was unfortunate, for when I saw Zalmné he stayed only briefly; just to say "Hello" and then he disappeared.

I followed the trail to the secluded beach, hoping to trace Suleman or Isabella? Suleman did not respond when I called for him. I continued to walk further along the beach and I saw Isabella's silhouette etched against the

STAR

MAGICIAN

sky-line; standing very erect and gazing out to sea in contemplation. She was dressed as a nun in a black and white habit and her feet were bare. I was pleased to see her; I liked her serene manner. She filled me with her warmth and her love oozed into my heart. We did not speak, but held hands and strolled leisurely along the shore. Mysteriously, out of the sands a ghostly cobra emerges snaking this way and that. It seemed to move in my insides and I was gradually aware of becoming the snake.

I was a serpent slithering on the dry sand and I zigzagged on my soft belly to a dark musty wood; where the path was strewn with rotting leaves. I crawled onto the rough bark of a tree. I felt an enormous power within. It was as if I was Medusa, masterful and invincible. The whole sphere was mine.

After the power of the kundalini had passed through my body; Isabella signalled for us to return to the beach. When we got there, we were joined by my female Shadow. She was naked except for an elaborate one inch, gold band around the circumference of her head. It was decorated with birds in flight, and in its centre was a sparkling ruby. After a warm greeting she said, "Come."

We went into the forest and under a giant conifer, we stopped. My Shadow stretched her arms out wide and communed silently with her creatures. An owl, an eagle and a parrot flew in and landed on her arms. We continued our journey and when we came to a cave she announced, "This is my home." She lit a fire and the semi-darkness turned to a bright orange. The atmosphere was warm and pleasant and we sat and talked.

In wonder I said, "Your life in the inner world is a whole lot better than mine. I like the way you commune with the beasts in the forest. How is it possible?"

"Once you have the mastery of life within your grasp anything is possible. There is no limit to the imagination and what can be imagined can be achieved."

Then I asked Isabella to bathe me in sea water as I felt drained and heavy. She poured water over my head and I felt soothed and refreshed. Afterwards I said farewell and returned to my physical body.

Date of meditation: 29/12/91 8.00 AM

SELF REALISATION

I did not see Zalmné at the pool so I took the path leading to the secluded beach. I sat idly on a large grey rock and cast round white pebbles into the swishing sea, and wished for nicer things for the future. Suleman appeared, emerging from the mists of time. I glanced at him and noted the details of his fine garments.

He wore a gold satin turban with a flashing crimson ruby surrounded by white dove feathers. Long silk multi-coloured tassels hung from his shoulders. His knee-length tunic was of a heavy white satin, and fastened with mother-of-pearl buttons. His loose pants were heavily embroidered with delicate coloured silk threads. On his feet he wore white satin slippers.

I confided,"I have a problem concerning my private life."

He said, "Come with me, I will take you to see Old Pan. He will help you."

We flew on Suleman's unicorn to the Devil's home. We stopped inside his foul cavern where we found him engaging in his usual lustful activity. His ugly face repulsed me. He looked at me ferociously and demanded, "What do you want?"

"I have come to ask your advice about a worldly matter."

He replied, "Drink some of the sweet wine I gave you."

I drank some of the cool liquid from the silver chalice, and placed the cold hard chalice against forehead my to ease the niggling worry in my head. It worked immediately, the nagging tension dissipated.

Feeling better, I asked, "What can I do to cure this problem once and for all?"

"Do not dwell on it, instead have faith and patience and everything will work out."

We left the dark smelly cavern and flew in the silver clouds. In mid-flight, I questioned; "Can you help me in curing my self-imposed loneliness?"

My guide replied, "The Hermit and World are responsible for causing your dilemma. I will take you to them."

We flew to the Hermit's home in the heart of the forest. Once there, my guide called for the World to come and join us. The Hermit was sitting on his wooden box as usual and the World came as before. Suleman addressed both of them: "Your energies are unbalanced within this individual. You must endeavour to be more conscious of each other and work in harmony and co-operation. At least, try to understand, you are both to blame for the distress in the psyche of this person."

They agreed at once and instantly, their blockage began to clear inside me.

After the two archetypes left, Suleman offered the information, "The Hermit in you is very powerful. You possess many of its traits. The planet Vulcan is fast approaching and it has a sole purpose which is to accelerate growth and the awakening of a new spirituality within you."

He carried on expounding, "Your life now lies like an empty shell and you feel loneliness all around you. All the living seem dead, and yet, you feel an invisible hand guiding you to your destiny. The grief of separation from your father at an early age and your two disastrous marriages, have

THE
MOON

THE TWINS

aggravated the sense of alienation within you."

"What shall I do then?" I wailed in desolate despair. "Do nothing," he stated. "Be like the sea, and take an example from it. Let the tides of life ebb and flow as they will. Be the observer of these events and learn from them. Let each second drift along its course, and remember each moment of your day is precious. Do not let despondency cloud your judgement. There is much to achieve before all is fulfilled." Slowly and sincerely I remarked, "It is so beautiful here. Why can't I stay here forever? It is becoming increasingly more difficult to break the barrier of the inner and outer spheres."

Kindly, he explained,"Your ego has become enchanted with these dimensions, and it is in conflict with itself. It is a difficult task you have undertaken." I said farewell and returned rather quickly to rejoin my body; as I wanted to write all of it down.

Date of meditation: 30/12/91

SPHERE OF KETHER

THE HEALING

I walked into the dim shadowy light of the cave and went straight across to the other entrance facing me. I surveyed the scene for several seconds and clambered down the uneven gravel paths leading to the secluded beach.

I saw ghostly forms on horseback racing along the deserted shore, and I called for my guide to come to me. Like a hazy mirage swirling in opaque mists, my Chindar stood beside me.

I watched him closely, admiring his attire. He wore a thigh-length loose shirt in a creamy-white shantung silk and a turban in a deep shade of pink; one end of the silky material fell over his left shoulder at the front and gently billowed in the breeze. His pants ballooned at the ankles and were made in a shiny pale-pink satin. He looked truly magnificent, sitting astride his chestnut-coloured mare.

We went to one of his caves in the wilderness and sat by the glowing fire and conversed. A little apprehensively I said, "I am beside myself, ghosts from the past haunt me. Vivid recollections flood my memory and I am full of intangible remorse. Why? What is the remedy?"

"Come, we will meet the Tower and Old Pan, who are responsible for this dilemma." We rode across the inner plains looking for them. The Tower came into view as before, like King Arthur. The Devil was the same, he never changes. We stood near to each other in silence, not holding hands. My guide, the two archetypes and I, rode to King Arthur's castle.

97

I addressed King Arthur, "Can you explain to me the reason for my peculiar sadness about the past?"

He held the mighty Excalibur in his right hand and exclaimed, "I will cut away the diseased part of you. Your anguish will vanish." He thrust the hard steel deep into my soft heart. I could feel its power penetrating my psyche, cleansing my great sorrow.

Then the Devil offered his advice, "To cure the self, take a sip of the sweet wine." I took a gulp from the silver goblet and as soon as it touched my lips, it dissolved my deep pain.

"What is it you need from me for your help?" I asked them both.

No one replied. There was a long silence then the Tower said, "Old Pan and I have healed you. In return, we ask you to be kind and considerate to other people." I promised to comply with their request. The Devil then spoke. "You have to extract the goodness of the sweet wine and give it away to others."

Chindar and I left them and returned to the serene beach. I climbed to the top of the hill and back into the cave. We said farewell and I kissed him lightly before I stepped inside. Soon, I rejoined my body sitting patiently in meditation.

Date of meditation: 31/12/91

NOTHING CHANGES

Today, the inner perceptions were very lucid. I saw Zalmné waiting at the pool, and strangely, as we walked through the forest, I saw a bewitching white goose. It followed us. I also saw a brown and white flecked fawn.

I lay down to rest in the hammock, and for the first time really scrutinised my own astral body. I grinned to myself as I looked at my funny toes and the fresh growth of coarse prickly hair sprouting on my shins. Moving up, I saw the dark brown scar-marks on my knobbly knees and the small upraised mole on my abdomen. I saw the whole of me with all the imperfections. It was an alien sensation to say the least, but nevertheless marvellous. My body felt light and ephemeral.

I sauntered over to the pool, Zalmné appeared again astride his white stallion. His mood was cheerful; not sullen as it was normally. He took my hand and pulled me up. He wore only a very brief loin-cloth, barely covering his genitals. It was nice to be with him and I held him close, thinking, I love him so.

He was quite talkative which was very unusual and we discussed several matters which were on my mind. I enquired in concern, "What is to be done about my problems?"

"Do nothing," he replied, "everything shall fall into place at the right time."

I trusted his judgement wholeheartedly. In the past when I had sought his advice, everything had fallen into place smoothly and mysteriously.

"Where are we going now?"

"We are going to the beach." It was extremely pleasant riding with him and I was aware of being at one with him.

"It is so peaceful here." I commented, "it seems like heaven."

"The inner-land is not free of its monstrosities." he stated simply. "The inner guides possess the power to ward off evil entities." I had wondered, why my path had been free of ugly demons and ferocious animals.

We stopped at a cave at the edge of the beach and the green sea-water was gently breaking at its entrance. We walked in. It was dry inside and we sat down on the sand and talked.

For the first time I asked candidly. "Why is there never any sex between us?"

"We are not here for the physical act of loving. I am here to teach you of the spiritual source of being."

He handed me a shimmering, translucent, white, silk dress, saying, "Put it on and go and stand at the sea edge."

I did as he asked. I became as vibrant as the sea-air. The dress whipped and billowed about in the cool fresh breeze. I was in the bliss of God; and as I turned my head to face the sun, I saw that Lord Gabriel was beside me. He was wearing a white robe of a flimsy silk and a dark-red sash-around his waist. He had huge transparent crimson wings. He said, "I am taking you on a heavenly trip."

I was conscious of Zalmné being with us. I held on tight to Lord Gabriel's left hand and Zalmné's right hand and this way we levitated upwards into a pellucid sky flying towards the, large spherical magenta disc setting on the misty horizon, aflame with amber fire, touched by pink and grey hazy hues.

We were drifting in a. mystifying new light, iridescent, stupefying and unbearable almost to the point of excruciating ecstasy. In delirium I enquired. "Will I experience this sensation after I have died? Will I ever see you again, Zalmné?"

"After death nothing changes. I will be here and all will be the same. Your body will whither but your spirit will not."

"You seem so real to me." I heard myself saying, "I even miss you in my mortal world, I think of you every day."

"As long as you love and need me, I will be here, and even after death, I will still exist."

Lord Gabriel left us and we flew towards the forest. On the way we stopped at the lake to see the High Priestess. When she appeared I said to her, "Heal my bladder, it is sore." She produced a laser-wand and touched the organ, explaining, "It will be better soon."

We carried on through the forest and when I saw the Fool coiling between the trees, with the luminous creatures of the forest, dancing above his head, I became aroused. A familiar throbbing spread in my lower pelvic region. His transparent body held me in a tender caress. Eroticism coursed in our veins and we embraced passionately. I thrust myself against him. My stomach muscle tensed as I gasped in pain then moaned in sheer delight. His lips brushed mine. I surrendered to the orgasmic-spasm; my whole body tingled. I felt as if I had become one with the stars and the heavens.

Afterwards Zalmné and I rode towards the clearing. I waved goodbye to the Fool as he disappeared back into the forest. I touched the outside wall of the cave and stepped inside to reunite with my body.

Date of meditation: 8/1/92

SUCH JOY

I stepped inside the cave, straightaway, I went over to the entrance facing me. I perused the golden sunlight pouring onto the hillside. The beach below was deserted.

I pondered whether to go down, or to go the other way to the forest. I decided on the latter and called the spiritual dove.

"Oh Come Spiritual Dove,
Come rest on my arm,
Take me to my Inner Guide,
So I am free from any harm."

It came and I followed it. Zalmné was not waiting for me at the Autumn pool, so I carried on walking to the secluded beach. I called all my guides in turn, without success. I felt lonely and was on the verge of being afraid so I decided to retrace my steps back to the pool. Just as I was about to leave Zalmné appeared, but not as a man but as a fresh-faced youth. We did not speak, just acknowledged each other with our eyes and our looks. We sat down in a yoga-fashion and contemplated.

The first to arrive on the scene was the High Priestess as Lady Mary. She was dressed in a magnificent golden robe with a wide hood hiding her head and face. She let me hold the baby and I cried with elation.

The Fool arrived next and then the Sun. We sat on the grass-verge near the pool and were silent for a. long time. I was churning over my worldly problems, trying to pluck up courage to ask for advice. The atmosphere between us all was charged like that preceding a storm. Suddenly, I saw a dazzling clear light. To my surprise, I could touch it. I revelled in this new experience. The crystal light blazed before my eyes illuminating every aspect of my being. I felt it vibrate within me, uniting me with the an unknown power.

As though from a far distance, I heard my guide speaking: "You are in the Sphere of Kether." I really did not want to leave this plane, and had to tear myself away.

I walked to the cave, went inside and returned reluctantly to my meditating body.

Date of meditation: 19/2/92

DIVINE BRILLIANCE

I stepped inside the cave and went over to the other entrance. I called for Chindar, as I surveyed the seascape. My view to my left was obscured, but to my right, I saw the magenta sun, a massive glimmering haze, low on the misty horizon. The shadows were opalescent and silver-grey and cast resplendent lights on the shimmering waves.

Chindar did not respond to my call so I retreated inside the cave and touched the wall on my left. I moved into the inner-landscape and stood before the clearing and summoned the dove, then, followed it in the forest. Zalmné was not at the Autumn pool, .so I walked further to the secluded beach. There was still no response from any guide so I stood alone on the seashore. Then I saw a vision.

A man in a white robe was hovering over the sea. His wispy blonde hair blew wildly in the breeze. I was beginning to be afraid when I sensed Chindar standing behind me. I enquired, "Who is that person?"

He replied, "It is the Strength, another of your guide on the path. He has something to show you." Then the strange figure vanished into the thin air and a. fine clear light lit the sky. The sea caught fire and gigantic golden flames rose from it. Silver shooting stars cascaded across the heavens and a dazzling divine brilliance spread across their expanse. I was captivated by this magnificent sight and surrendered myself to it. Words cannot describe it.

I asked, "Where am I?"

Chindar replied, "You are in the Sphere of Kether. "

I revelled as waves of intense pleasure swept over me. An unseen force filled my body, gradually moving upwards from my toes to my knees, to my thighs, to my vaginal cavity, stomach, heart, lungs, larynx, forehead and finally it touched my crown. A white light exploded in my head and across the heavens and expanding out into space and to the other dimensions.

"You are united with the supreme God." I heard Chindar say. In an explosion of the intense blue-white light, I felt the kundalini begin to flutter in my belly. It moved and a warm suffusing rush of love spread inside me satisfying every part of my soul.

I relaxed once more in the Realms of Kether. The divine form moved

and breathed over me. The power of the kundalini pulsated in my belly
Deep within my body and mind, the power throbbed. In the clear light all the
mysteries dissolved. For a brief moment time and space merged and I was at one
with the universe, nothing was hidden from me.

Date of meditation: 24/2/92

THE WHITE EXPLOSION

I was listening to the tape, Atlantis, and I moved directly to the Autumn pool.
Zalmné stood statue-like in deep contemplation. He was naked. I watched him
intently; almost hypnotised, drawn to his strange power. An adder slid over his
bare skin. In my own body, I felt the kundalini moving in my toes, snaking
upwards to cleanse all the major chakras. All the gifts' powers vibrated in me,
revealing the hidden secrets. I was profoundly aware of the precious knowledge.
The kundalini moved like lightning. Great surges of electricity rushed like
quicksilver through my body. Then unexpectedly, my guide and I were flying
through the heavens. A ghostly python appeared in the sky before us. We sat
astride its massive back and it carried us into the brilliant-white exploding light.
Words are inadequate to describe what I saw. Blue stars and the red mass
whirled around me. Then the red masses separated in millions of smaller masses
each spinning rapidly, forming smaller bright spheres. I knew I was witnessing
the creation itself.

Date of meditation: 14/3/92

BEING WITH GOD

I was listening to the tape, Temple in the Forest. Touching the wall of the cave
I entered the inner-landscape. Feeling as light as air, I followed the dove, and
listened to the birds twitter overhead.

Zalmné was not waiting for me, so I carried on towards the beach. I peered
inside Suleman's cavern, but he was not there.

I went near the sea and sat down on the golden sand, listening to the seagulls
screech overhead and waited patiently for a guide to appear. From the distance,
the sound of thunderous hooves came nearer, pounding hard on the beach. I
turned around and saw Chindar mounted on his galloping unicorn, heading in
my direction.

He stopped and dismounted. After the greetings we sat in contemplative
meditation. The unicorn nuzzled me and touched me gently with its golden
horn.

Date of meditation: 16/3/92

THE BETTER WORLD

I stepped inside the cave and without any hesitation walked straight across to entrance opposite and watched the silver clouds scudding in the sheet-blue sky. I called for my guide Chindar and he appeared. We clambered down the rock-strewn gravel paths to the beach and waited patiently for someone to come. Shortly, a man came. He wore a long dazzling white cotton robe and a lengthy veil which hid his face. He carne forward and straightaway announced, "I am the one you seek."

I stared at him stupidly and blankly There was something about him.

I sensed a greater power than I had ever experienced before.

I offered him my right hand in greeting. On contact I knew I held the hand of the Supreme Being.

He said, "Yes, I am the First, and the Last, the Beginning and the End. I am the Infinity, the Past, Present and Future."

I asked, "Why have I been fortunate enough to meet you?"

"Because you have searched for me."

"After death, will I be born again in the New World?"

"I have many kingdoms and you will enter one of them."

"What about reincarnation?"

"It is the same thing."

"The same thing?"

"The Soul will live for ever."

"There are so many religions, which one is right? Is there one true path? I am confused, God, Allah, Jehovah, which one are you?"

"I am all of them, to worship in love is to worship me. The name is immaterial, as long as the prayers are from the heart. Go now, but come and meet me again."

Date of meditation: 11/4/92

I understand now that my life is fulfilled for God has spoken to me. By his mystery, I know He is for ever-more; and in my heart I will pray for you, that you will find Him as I have done, and that you will search for the secret storehouse of knowledge and wisdom that can be found in meditation.

I have decided to stop writing at this point, but I will continue to explore by meditating. I will carry on with the spiritual exploration and I hope my account of my own search will touch your heart, and encourage you to embark on your own journey.

May the God of all of us bless you. May inner peace and solace brighten your day.

Date of final collation: 9/8/92

Jason Simpson
Copyright 1993